FOR MY DEAR DAD, DAVID,
WHO, IN ALL HONESTY,
WOULD PROBABLY RATHER
GO FLY-FISHING THAN
HAVE A PARTY.

ALICE HART

FRIENDS AT MY TABLE

PHOTOGRAPHY BY EMMA LEE

Quadrille
PUBLISHING

07 Introduction | 10 Seasonality chart
12 Equipment and techniques to cook for crowds

SPRING

14 Vietnamese bridal shower | 30 Vegetarian garden brunch
44 Holiday weekend away

Summer

62 Laid-back country wedding | 84 Glamping
96 Beach cricket barbecue

AUTUMN

108 A chic, easy picnic | 120 Harvest festival lunch
130 Firepit night

WINTER

144 Help yourself New Year's Eve supper
162 Cosy weekend away | 174 Mezze night

188 Extra helpings | 190 Index | 192 Acknowledgements

FOOD, SETTING AND NOSTALGIA ARE SO KEENLY INTERTWINED. Unsurprising, perhaps, when one

considers how the milestones peppering our lives are marked with celebrations and gatherings. Keeping such merrymaking and a generous number of guests in mind, this is a book of menus, recipes and advice to assist when cooking for those jolly occasions, be they humble, fanciful or downright elaborate.

I can think of few more rewarding occupations than cooking a supper, lunch or brunch for a good crowd of loved ones. Moreover, I hope that within these pages you will find techniques and steers to make life – and your enjoyment of the bash – that much easier.

We, the enthusiastic eaters and the cooks of today, have undeniably well-informed tastes. This doesn't mean that the recipes we cook should be complicated. The most important thing is always that the food be delicious, but if dishes can also be appealing in colour and contrasting in texture, you will be on to a winner. Using both the food and the changing seasons to help create a warm atmosphere – a sense of occasion, if you like – makes a party memorable without breaking the bank.

The recipes and menus in this book are temperate, balanced and well-suited to the unpredictable game of party-throwing. Cooking for larger numbers might seem daunting but, really, it needn't. Last-minute frying, slicing and dicing sends me into a tailspin; instead I'll throw in every simple technique I know to prep in advance and get ahead, safe in the knowledge that supper is in hand. It takes a certain adjustment to think in terms of hearty, bountiful, and often family-style dishes, rather than anything fiddly or fussy. These are intended to be happy, relaxed occasions and what would be the point in inviting friends over if you didn't get to down tools early, pick up a glass of something fizzy and enjoy yourself? List makers rejoice, for this is your time. A simple battle strategy, some forward planning and a few lists will help keep you on track.

From a small-but-chic country wedding to a bountiful New Year's Eve spread, via spring brunch and weekends away with friends, the emphasis on seasonality throughout these chapters is not just for show, it will also help to create a fitting atmosphere. Embrace the whimsy each changing month of the year has to offer and use it to your advantage. The message has truly hit home now: food in season bursts with flavour. In addition, said bounty is nearly always cheaper and has a higher nutritional value than its off-season relations, so take advantage of any gluts you find at the markets. If you are making a recipe at a different time of year than originally intended, substitute like-for-like vegetables or fruit – root for root, berry for berry – and perhaps have a test run in advance; there are plenty of suggestions for alternative ingredients in the recipe introductions.

Getting the best value from a joint of meat, a magnificent fish or a crate of fruit is paramount, especially when forking out on larger quantities for a special occasion. Brining and smokily roasting, say, a hefty slab of silverside to make a great quantity of spiced pastrami, as in the New Year chapter you'll find here, takes so much pressure off the cook as all the preparation happens in the preceding week. Shaving the pastrami into slices, to serve on rye bread with mustard, pickles and winter salad leaves will stretch a handsome, yet relatively thrifty, piece of beef an awfully long way.

The best advice I can give you in all this is to keep a calm head. Try not to run yourself ragged, or abandon a recipe simply because you can't locate a particular ingredient. Instead, make a logical and seasonal substitution. Similar herbs, cuts of meat, fish and full-fat dairy are usually interchangeable, as long as you use a dash of common sense and don't stray too far from the original. Have faith in your taste buds though; if you can't find kaffir lime leaves, chuck in some lime zest and don't give it another thought. You are in charge of this food and not the other way around!

I have catered for events, large and small, cheffed in pubs and restaurants and private houses, run baking stalls, cooked hundreds and hundreds of recipes for glossy photoshoots and written and developed even more for print. Two nuggets of wisdom I have gleaned are, firstly, to shop and prepare in advance – in fact, as far in advance as is humanly possible – and, secondly, to spread the workload out, rather than expecting to get everything done on the day. As I'll show you, many of the cunning techniques chefs employ when preparing food for large crowds prove incredibly useful to the home cook, but none as much as assembling a 'mise en place', where, if the entire dish can't be finished before the day, the ingredients are chopped or partially cooked ahead, ready to be put together to order. You will find few pyrotechnics in this book, no wildly difficult techniques or finickety sauces, but, as I point out in the relevant recipes, feeding 10, 16, or even 20 well requires forethought, and I can guide you through. I'm not suggesting for a minute that you cook in such volumes every day; I certainly don't. However, I'm used to, and relaxed about, cooking for large numbers. With the right recipes, cooking for 10 rather than two can be just as easy, and you might as well make a real night of it.

There would be little point in a cookbook that won't be useful and usable to a broad range of readers, so a balance had to be found in the party sizes. There are menus for not-so-daunting groups of six, right up to menus for 20, but, apart from a sumptuous strawberry and vanilla wedding cake to feed the five thousand, that was the point at which I stopped. Most recipes can be halved or quartered if needed and, where suitable, I have tried to indicate this in the text. Don't be afraid to make a larger quantity, as written, and freeze the remainder for another time. You'll probably thank your kind and organised self in the future when you need an instant supper or dessert.

A real advantage of catering for large numbers is that the more people you have to feed, the less you have to make. What I mean is, there's a magical point at which the finished quantities seem to stretch themselves. You might expect, quite logically, that a recipe for four could be multiplied by four to serve 16... but no. In reality, there will be enough food for 18, perhaps even more. Recipe multiplication is a fickle beast, but at least it errs on the side of generosity, which is surely the key to a great party.

The 12 menus here, three for each season, have been carefully tested and balanced to suit the occasion, season and party size, but if one look at them fills you with terror, have no shame at all in cherry-picking what you can cope with and simplifying or delegating the rest. Serve fresh fruit and bought ice cream for pudding; draft in help from friends and family; delegate an entire course to somebody else; serve a simple salad and some lovely bread with a main course and leave it at that.

It takes a certain arrogance to assume that you will follow like a lamb and make everything on a suggested menu. Each recipe should stand proud and alone, so of course you are encouraged to cook them on their own, without their accompanying dishes. Making a menu in its entirety, however, shouldn't cause any problems regarding the different timings, oven temperatures and oven space called for. I often move some of the cooking outside, to take the pressure off the kitchen. Building your own firepit or hot smoker outdoors may not fall into the category of upright entertaining (a distinct plus, 'entertaining' being a hateful word anyway), but it will make cooking that majestic joint of meat or clutch of root vegetables exciting and earthy, while including your friends in the process.

All this wining and dining goes beyond getting food on the table and I hope you will glean some relevant, and decidedly non-Stepford, ideas to help in pushing that boat out in a variety of settings. I would rarely bother to set tables rigidly for example: cutlery piled into jars and set on the table for people to help themselves looks charming and will save you considerable fuss. There is no rule saying chairs, crockery and tables need to match or that seating arrangements can't be on the cosy side... so relax and have fun with it all.

Gathering friends and family together to eat, drink and make merry need not feel like a test or an exercise in stress; the main aim is that everybody has a good time. Including you.

SEASONALITY CHART

When fruits, herbs and vegetables are at their best, based on UK (and Northern Europe)

SPRING

ALPHONSO MANGO | ASPARAGUS | BROCCOLI CAULIFLOWER | CELERIAC | CHICORY | CHIVES CUCUMBER | DILL | LEEK | SALADS (*early*) PARSLEY | PASSION FRUIT | PURPLE-SPROUTING BROCCOLI | RADISH | RHUBARB | SPINACH | SPRING ONION STRAWBERRY (*early*)| TARRAGON

Summer

APRICOT | ARTICHOKE | AUBERGINE | BEETROOT BASIL | BLACKBERRY | BLACKCURRANT BLUEBERRY | BOK CHOI AND PAK CHOI BROAD BEAN | BROCCOLI | CARROT | CELERY CHERRY | CHERVIL | CHILLI | CHIVES | CORIANDER | COURGETTE CUCUMBER | DILL | FIG | FLORENCE (*bulb*) FENNEL | GARLIC GOOSEBERRY | SALADS (*summer*) | MANGETOUT | MELON | MINT MULBERRY | NEW POTATO | ONION AND SHALLOT | OREGANO PARSLEY | PEA AND SUGARSNAP PEA | PLUM | POTATO (*maincrop*) RADISH | RASPBERRY | REDCURRANT | RHUBARB | ROCKET ROSEMARY | SAGE | SPINACH | SPRING ONION | STRAWBERRY SWEETCORN | TARRAGON | TOMATO | THYME | TURNIP WATERCRESS | WILD MUSHROOM

AUTUMN APPLE | BEETROOT | BLACKBERRY
BUTTERNUT SQUASH | CARROT | CELERIAC
CELERY | CHICORY | CHIVES | FIG | FLORENCE
(*bulb*) FENNEL | GARLIC | GRAPE | HAZELNUT
HORSERADISH | JERUSALEM ARTICHOKE | KALE | KOHLRABI
LEEK | SALADS (*late*) | NECTARINE | ONION AND SHALLOT
PARSLEY | PARSNIP | PEACH | PEAR | PEPPER | PINEAPPLE
PLUM | POTATO (*maincrop*) | PUMPKIN | RADISH | RASPBERRY
ROCKET | ROSEMARY | SAGE | SPRING ONION | SWEETCORN
TARRAGON | TOMATO | THYME | WATERCRESS
WILD MUSHROOM | WINTER SQUASH

WINTER BEETROOT | BLOOD ORANGE | CAULIFLOWER
CELERIAC | CELERY | CHICORY | HORSERADISH
JERUSALEM ARTICHOKE | KALE | LEEK
LEMON | MANGO | ONION AND SHALLOT
ORANGE | PASSION FRUIT | PARSNIP | POMEGRANATE
POTATO (*maincrop*) | PUMPKIN | PURPLE-SPROUTING BROCCOLI
RADISH | ROSEMARY | RHUBARB | SAGE | SPRING ONION
THYME | TURNIP | WILD MUSHROOM | WINTER SALADS (*until first
frosts unless protected*) | WINTER SQUASH

Food safety is something to bear in mind constantly when cooking for larger numbers. It is obviously of paramount importance that food, especially meat, be cooked adequately, and it can be easier to miss when you have large quantities or multiples to deal with, or when using alternative and slow-cooking methods, such as smoking. I use a **MEAT THERMOMETER**, just to make sure. Stick it into the centre of the meat and adhere to the following:

	VERY RARE-RARE	MEDIUM	WELL DONE
BEEF, LAMB AND VENISON	45-50°C	60°C	70°C
PORK	N/A	70°C	75°C
POULTRY	N/A	N/A	82°C (min. temp.)
GAME BIRDS	N/A	74°C (min. temp.)	above 74°C

An **OVEN THERMOMETER** is also essential. Most ovens run hot or cool, or have hot spots; you might not even realise your oven is actually at a different temperature to that indicated on the dial. When you've spent more time and effort on larger quantities of ingredients, it would be especially heartbreaking to scorch them through no fault of your own, so buy an oven thermometer – they are reasonably priced and widely available in cooking shops and supermarkets – and adhere to its temperature reading, rather than your oven dial.

It will involve some pretty hefty expenditure, but if you're really serious about getting some fast prep done, a **FOOD PROCESSOR** will help you out no end. It's a somewhat contentious method (the purists would say always use your hands), but I use mine to make shortcrust pastry in batches.

It takes mere minutes and, if you are careful to use the pulse button and not overwork the flour, produces chilled, short results every time. Thicker slicing, rough chopping, batter mixing, sauces and mayonnaise can all be churned out in a food processor with very little bother. I would highly recommend the KitchenAid make for their sturdiness and good looks. The same goes for their free-standing food mixer, but if you are watching the pennies, a good compromise would be...

...An **ELECTRIC HAND WHISK** – a heavy-duty model rather than something too cheap and flimsy – will do you great service for smoothly whipping up batters, meringues, cream and the like.

The largest **ROASTING TINS** and **BAKING TRAYS** that will fit into your oven. If possible, they should be sturdy enough to sit on the hob, for making gravies and sauces after roasting.

EXTRA-WIDE FOIL or turkey foil. The thick sort, not the cheap, thin sort that tears if you so much as look at it. For lidding and roasting.

Non-stick **BAKING PAPER** and **CLING FILM**, for baking without greasing tins and for covering food made in advance, respectively. If you don't want to buy cling film, use upturned plates and baking sheets to cover bowls and dishes. It is terribly useful when wrapping pastry and covering bowls of rising bread dough, though.

A big **COLANDER**. For draining rice or pasta, potatoes or noodles, or for rinsing.

A really large stockpot-type **SAUCEPAN** with a lid. For making soups and stocks on the stovetop. A big Le Creuset-style casserole is also invaluable.

A very long **WOODEN SPOON** and ladle. For the stockpot saucepan.

A good supply of heavy-duty and large **CHOPPING BOARDS**. A few, if possible, so you can chop different food groups hygienically and save washing up until you have finished prepping.

Large springform **CAKE TINS**, tart tins with removable bases and pie dishes. Obviously, this depends greatly on what you will be baking but I consider anything above 23cm in diameter to be large. You can hire cake tins from cake decorating shops if you would rather not buy them. You might want to cook a cake in a different-shaped tin; in which case the following is good to know: square tins hold about one-quarter more again of the quantity as round tins of the same size. So, cooking times will increase for square tins, but the oven temperature should remain the same. These tins will hold the same amount of batter:

20cm round = 18cm square
23cm round = 20cm square
28cm round = 26cm square

A big, heavy-based, non-stick or cast-iron **FRYING PAN**. Spend as much as you can afford on a great frying pan. You will use it all the time and for everything.

Food-safe, **PLASTIC CONTAINERS** with lids for storing, transporting and marinating. They aren't pretty. Hide them in a cupboard.

At least a couple of really big **PLASTIC MIXING BOWLS**. You can pick these up very cheaply. Again, they are not attractive and you won't want to show them off, but they are incredibly useful for tossing salads, marinating, brining, mixing batters and dough...

SPARE TABLES. Trestle tables or foldaway tables are just fine. Cover them with tablecloths if they are less than beautiful.

For blitzing soups, vegetables and sauces in their saucepans, you'll need a **HAND BLENDER**. To be perfectly honest, I am wedded to my lovely (safe) free-standing blender, due in part to a minor accident with a hand blender a few years ago. However, if the price of an upright blender is prohibitive, a hand blender is a fantastic thing. Do switch it off at the mains when you finish using it.

A **MANDOLIN**, as extolled in the Holiday Weekend Away chapter, will prove its worth if you ever make potatoes à la dauphinoise or shredded salads for more than two. A good-value, plastic model will be more than adequate.

If you have a birthday, wedding or anniversary present due and you are a fan of all things sweet and frozen, an **ICE CREAM MAKER** is the thing to hint at. I have a deep love for mine and it makes short work of whipping up delectable, smooth ices with none of that incessant 'beating every two hours until set' business. Pour in your chilled base mix, switch it on, and you should have pudding in 20 minutes or so. The results make a mockery of over-priced tubs. The only negatives are the whirring noise (I frequently sit mine in another room and close the door while it churns) and the sheer weight of the thing, but we must bear such crosses in return for good ice cream.

A NOTE ON THESE RECIPES
* Spoon measurements are level, unless stated.
* If not specified, butter should be salted.
* Eggs are large, unless stated. Do please buy free-range. I favour Clarence Court's pale blue Cotswold Legbar eggs, for the deep orange yolks.
* The recipes have been tested using whole milk and full-fat dairy, unless stated.
* 'Salt' refers to flakes of sea salt; 'pepper' refers to freshly ground black peppercorns.
* Ovens run at varying temperatures. The recipes were tested using a thermometer for accuracy.

VIETNAMESE BRIDAL SHOWER FOR 8

BEEF IN BETEL LEAVES | **STICKY QUAIL IN HONEY & FIVE SPICE** | *Green mango salad* | VIETNAMESE TABLE SALAD AND PICKLED VEGETABLES | BAKED WHITE CHOCOLATE & RHUBARB CUSTARDS | PINEAPPLE AND GINGER FIZZ

The bridal theme is merely a suggestion; this dainty menu would be a dream for any spring supper. Haphazard and charming might not be your thing, but it certainly makes for a pretty table. Cutlery and chopsticks can amassed in a pot in the middle, or tied loosely with twine at each place setting. Nothing needs to match.

Spring blooms, herbs and tea lights in jam jars look beautiful; basil and lemon verbena will both smell delicious and ward off evening bugs to boot. If you have the wherewithal to eat outside, fairy lights threaded through greenery or a few paper lanterns on the ground never go amiss.

Spread the preparation over a couple of days to make things easier on yourself. The custards can be made two days ahead, as can the pickles and dipping sauce (which doubles as a salad dressing). The salads come to no harm if put together an hour or two before serving and kept, covered, in a cool place.

Despite all this, I suggest getting some help from a willing minion. Although nothing is particularly complicated, there is rather a lot of chopping and shredding. Such is usually the way with south east Asian dishes. Soldier on, however, and you will be duly rewarded with an exceptional supper.

Instead of serving everything savoury at once, as intended, you could start with the beef and treat the quail as a main with the green mango salad. For vegetarians, separately marinate cubes of firm tofu in the quail marinade for a few hours. Roast in a moderate oven, turning now and then, until golden and sticky. Knock up an extra dipping sauce using light soy in place of fish sauce. It won't be the same, but it will be no less delicious.

BEEF IN BETEL LEAVES
(BO LA LOT)

MAKES ABOUT 48 (6 EACH)
PREP 30 MINUTES
COOK 10 MINUTES

5 tbsp peanuts, toasted and
   crushed or chopped
700g coarsely minced beef
2 garlic cloves, very finely
   chopped
2 lemon grass stalks, bulbous
   ends only, very finely chopped
3 spring onions, white parts only,
   finely chopped (use the
   green parts for the quail,
   see page 21)
1 tsp curry powder
1 tbsp fish sauce
2 tsp caster sugar
½ tsp freshly ground white
   pepper
45-55 large betel leaves (you'll
   need 2 large bunches)

DARK GREEN, HEART-SHAPED BETEL LEAVES CAN BE FOUND IN THAI OR VIETNAMESE FOOD SHOPS. They will be nestling in chiller cabinets, wrapped in cellophane packets alongside the herbs. Use any duds in stir-fries and just concentrate on stuffing the large, unblemished leaves for your own sanity. While you're in the shop, look for Vietnamese (sometimes labelled 'Madras') curry powder. It's sweet, bright, highly fragrant and perfect with the beef.

Combine 3 tbsp of the crushed peanuts with all the remaining ingredients except the betel leaves. Season with a pinch of salt. Take a betel leaf and lay it shiny side-down on a work surface. Take 1 heaped dsp of the beef mixture, rolling it into a fat log. Place this on the pointed end of the betel leaf and roll up tightly, piercing the stalk end through the leaf to secure. This is nowhere near as tricky as it sounds, but the truly inept could use cocktail sticks. Repeat to make 48 rolls; you will get quicker and more dextrous as you go.

Place a large griddle or frying pan over a high heat. Griddle or fry the betel rolls in the pan – they won't stick – until slightly charred on all sides, in batches if necessary, keeping the cooked rolls warm in a low oven. The leaves will soften, wrinkle and turn shinier still. Serve about six per person, scattered with the remaining peanuts and sitting on a bed of rice noodles and Table Salad (see page 18).

VIETNAMESE DIPPING SAUCE
(NUOC CHAM)

MAKES ENOUGH FOR 8
PREP 5 MINUTES

4 tbsp caster sugar
6 tbsp rice wine vinegar
6 tbsp Vietnamese fish sauce
   (nuoc mam)
juice of 2 limes
2-3 Thai chillies, finely chopped,
   or to taste

THE UBIQUITOUS (IN VIETNAM, ANYWAY) *NUOC CHAM* IS BASED ON GOOD-QUALITY *NUOC MAM*, VIETNAMESE FISH SAUCE. Versions abound, but this one makes an excellent entry-level sauce to be adjusted to taste. Variations include adding finely chopped garlic and/or ginger and/or finely shredded pickled carrot and radish. It also doubles as a dressing for Asian salads.

Gently heat the sugar with the vinegar, fish sauce and 150ml water, until the sugar dissolves. Do not allow the mixture to boil. Let cool. Add the lime juice and chillies, depending on your preference for heat. Serve in little pots or dishes, or use as a salad dressing.

VIETNAMESE TABLE SALAD

MAKES ENOUGH FOR 8 AS AN ACCOMPANIMENT
PREP 10 MINUTES

250g fine rice noodles
small bunch of coriander
small bunch of mint
small bunch of Vietnamese mint
  or Thai basil (if available)
large handful of perilla
  (if available)
2 heads round lettuce, leaves
  separated, rinsed and dried
1 cucumber, sliced on the
  diagonal
1 starfruit, sliced (optional)
Pickled Vegetables (see below)
Nuoc Cham dipping sauce
  (see page 16)

A VIETNAMESE-STYLE TABLE SALAD IS THERE TO WRAP, roll and generally customise your supper. Use the larger lettuce leaves as vessels, filling them with any combination of rice noodles, fragrant herbs, a tangle of Pickled Vegetables (see below) and perhaps a slice of starfruit or cucumber. Add your main event – *Bo La Lot* or a boneless piece of quail in this case (see pages 16 and 21) – roll the leaf around the filling, then dip in Nuoc Cham and eat.

Soak the noodles in hot water for a few minutes, according to the packet instructions, then refresh under cold water and drain well.

Now either divide everything between individual serving bowls, keeping the components in groups rather than mixing them up, or serve on communal platters for your guests to help themselves.

PICKLED VEGETABLES

MAKES ENOUGH FOR 8 AS AN ACCOMPANIMENT
PREP 10 MINUTES

90g caster sugar
180ml rice vinegar
300g carrots, peeled and cut into
  fine matchsticks
200g daikon (white radish),
  peeled and cut into fine
  matchsticks

THESE QUICK PICKLES WILL KEEP, chilled, in their pickling bath for a good couple of weeks.

Combine the sugar and vinegar with 100ml water and a pinch of salt in a bowl, stirring until the sugar dissolves. Add the vegetable matchsticks and set aside for at least two hours to pickle them. Cover and refrigerate if you're going to keep them for longer.

Using your naturally favoured hand, hold one chopstick (near the top for added elegance), tucking it in between thumb and first finger so that the tip points diagonally downwards. Steady the stick further down towards the tip with the inside of your bent third finger.

Now add the second chopstick, holding it in the same place on the stick, grasping it as you would a pencil, so that both chopstick tips are at the same level. It should be held firmly between the tips of your thumb, index and middle fingers.

To pick up food, the index and middle fingers should pivot, bringing the second chopstick down to meet the first. Apply pressure with your thumb to hold the chopstick securely.

Practise moving the second chopstick freely, while the first chopstick remains stationary. Your movements will become more precise as you grow familiar with the sensation.

It is considered most impolite to 'spear' your food, so if all your attempts to be dextrous end in failure, better to give in and ask for a fork...

STICKY QUAIL IN HONEY AND FIVE SPICE (CHIME)

NOBODY IN THEIR RELAXED MIND WOULD OPT TO DEEP-FRY FOR EIGHT IN THE MIDDLE OF SUPPER, especially in a nice dress. So, on this occasion, I have recommended griddling the quail. They will take on beautiful charred tones and the skin will caramelise and become crisp.

If you are cooking this for supper rather than a party however, do try deep-frying the quails. Submerge three at a time in groundnut oil, patting them dry first. Check that the oil is hot with a scrap of bread; it should turn golden in about 30 seconds. Fry the little birds for about five minutes, until golden, drain well and serve hot. Incidentally, a platter of honeyed quails make a comely substitute for the humble burger in case you were looking for barbecue inspiration.

Using a pair of sharp scissors, snip through the backbone of each quail, opening out flat. Rinse under the tap and dry thoroughly with kitchen paper.

Grate the ginger finely, skin and all. Gather up the gratings and, holding your hands over a bowl, squeeze to release all the liquid. Discard the dry gratings. Add all the other marinade ingredients to the bowl, stir well and slather over the quails. Cover the bowl and set aside to chill for a few hours or overnight. A minimum of two hours will do, if that's all you have.

When ready to cook, heat the oven to 200°C/fan 180°C/400°F/gas mark 6 and line a large roasting tin with foil. Place a large griddle pan over a fierce heat until it's positively smoking. Working in two or three batches, shake the quails free of any excess marinade and griddle, skin side-down first, for a minute or so on each side, until burnished brown and charred in places. Transfer to the roasting tin, skin side up, as you go. When all have been griddled, pour any leftover marinade over the birds and roast for 10 minutes until just cooked through but still juicy. Meanwhile, mix together all the ingredients for the dipping sauce and place in a small bowl.

Pile the quails up on a platter, scatter with shredded spring onions and serve with the dipping sauce on the side.

SERVES 8
PREP 20 MINUTES, PLUS MARINATING
COOK ABOUT 12 MINUTES

8 quails
3 spring onions, green parts only, shredded

FOR THE MARINADE
thumb-sized piece of fresh root ginger
2½ tbsp dark soy sauce
2½ tbsp runny honey
2 garlic cloves, crushed
½ tsp five spice powder
2 tbsp Shaoxing rice wine

FOR THE LEMON AND PEPPER DIPPING SAUCE
juice of 2 lemons
2 tsp freshly ground white pepper
1 tsp sea salt

GREEN MANGO SALAD
(GOI XOAI XANH)

I COULD LIVE ON THIS. Customise as you wish with prawns, strips of pork belly, shredded chicken, roasted rice, fried shallots, crushed peanuts in place of the slightly inauthentic cashews, even dried shrimps or squid (found in Vietnamese grocers). As part of this menu, I've kept the components pure and simple.

If you find yourself in the aforementioned Vietnamese grocer, or any good Thai food shop, you can pick up a shredding tool very cheaply. They look like corrugated swivel peelers. If you don't have one, use the shredder attachment on a food processor, or peel the carrots and mango into thin strips with a vegetable peeler, then stack them into piles and slice into long matchsticks.

Make sure your Nuoc Cham has a good chilli kick, adding a finely sliced Thai chilli or two to remedy things should it fall short. Sweet, salt, sour and hot flavours should all be pronounced and balanced.

If your mangoes are very firm and dry, shred them into fine matchsticks. If they have any give at all when pressed, they will be too juicy for shredding, so slice or pare (using a swivel-blade vegetable peeler) into wide but delicate strips.

Combine all the ingredients except the cashews and set aside for 20 minutes or so before serving, so the flavours can get to know each other. Scatter with the nuts just before serving to add crunch.

SERVES 8
PREP 20 MINUTES

4 large green mangoes, peeled
2 carrots, scrubbed and finely shredded
handful of Vietnamese mint, Thai basil, mint or coriander, or a combination, shredded
6 tbsp Nuoc Cham dipping sauce (see page 16)
3 tbsp cashews, roasted and crushed

BAKED WHITE CHOCOLATE AND RHUBARB CUSTARDS

IF YOU HAVE THE TIME, MAKE THESE LIGHT AND WOBBLY CUSTARDS A DAY OR TWO BEFORE; it will spread the load. I've scented them with vanilla, but half a dozen cracked green cardamom pods will also marry beautifully with both the white chocolate and the rhubarb, should you wish to ring the changes.

The rhubarb leaves a stunning pink syrup behind; perfect as a base for drinks: top up with champagne, elderflower pressé or soda.

Preheat the oven to 200°C/fan 180°C/400°F/gas mark 6. Place the rhubarb in a roasting dish, scatter with the sugar, cover with foil and roast for 25 minutes, until tender but still holding its shape. Using a slotted spoon so most of the syrup is left behind, divide the rhubarb between eight ovenproof dishes, pots or ramekins, and chill.

Heat the cream, milk, salt and vanilla pod in a pan until steaming but not boiling. Remove from the heat and set aside to infuse for 20 minutes. Reduce the oven temperature to 170°C/fan 150°C/340°F/gas mark 3½. Chop 200g of the white chocolate quite finely and set the remainder aside. Return the cream mixture to the heat and bring up to just below boiling point, as before.

Whisk the egg yolks and sugar in a heatproof mixing bowl until pale and thickened. Remove the steaming pan from the heat and add the chopped chocolate, stirring to dissolve. Gradually pour this on to the egg yolks, whisking. Pass the mixture through a fine sieve into a jug to remove any strands of egg and the vanilla pod. (Rinse and dry the pod, then use it to flavour jars of sugar. You know the drill.)

Sit the rhubarb pots in a deep roasting tin. Very carefully pour the custard on to the rhubarb, slowly-slowly so as not to disturb the pink layer, filling to near the top, then cover each pot with a square of foil. Boil a kettle. Place the roasting tin in the middle of the oven, then pull the oven rack out and fill the tin with boiling water to reach halfway up each custard pot.

Bake for 35-40 minutes, until the custard is just set but still jiggles in the centre. Let cool, then chill for at least three hours or overnight.

Scrape a sharp knife, held at an angle, over the flat base of the reserved chocolate to make large shavings and scrolls. Pile these shavings messily on to each custard pot and serve.

SERVES 8
PREP 30 MINUTES
COOK 1 HOUR 15 MINUTES, PLUS
    20 MINUTES INFUSING AND AT
    LEAST 3 HOURS CHILLING

FOR THE RHUBARB
750g pink rhubarb, trimmed and
    chopped into 3cm lengths
125g golden caster sugar

FOR THE CUSTARDS
500ml single cream
250ml whole milk
pinch of salt
1 vanilla pod, split
300g white chocolate
6 egg yolks
3 tbsp golden caster sugar

Or, in other words, what I have learnt from attempting to cater from a domestic kitchen…

PLAN TO COOK VERY LITTLE FRIED FOOD

A few odds and ends are fine – a hot and crisp garnish for a salad perhaps – but anything more tends to mean a flustered, oil-spattered cook and kitchen, greasy food (because of the sheer quantities involved) and a general last-minute panic. Instead, use a low oven to braise and slowly roast. Toast nuts, seeds and bread in advance, to add crunch and a variety of textures.

TRY TO FREE UP THE OVEN FOR THE LAST 20 MINUTES OR SO

before you plan to eat, ready to be used for plate-warming, reheating and so on. Roasts should be tented with foil and left to rest; braises and stews will be volcanically hot, so a few minutes sitting on the work top with a lid on will not harm them. Try not to cook too many items – or any at all – that need to go from oven to plate with lightning speed.

USE YOUR FREEZER…

So much can be made and kept frozen until needed, even if it is just stocks and ice creams. Free up space in the fridge and the freezer, ready for the extra load. If necessary, beg, borrow, or hire extra room from a friend or neighbour. Temporary fridges and the like can be set up in a garage, barn, stable or shed with electrics. Incidentally, I keep large quantities of nuts and spices in the freezer to preserve their delicate oils.

DON'T OVERCOMPLICATE

Yes, be relatively ambitious and make that smoked pastrami or delightful chicken pie, but keep any extras simple. Let good food speak for itself.

PREPARE IN ADVANCE AND MAKE IN ADVANCE

When cooking for a crowd, never, ever leave everything until the last minute. Spread the prep out over a few days so that it doesn't feel so arduous, and make anything that won't suffer, or might even improve, ahead of time. Chopped onion and other vegetables can be stored in the fridge in airtight containers; dressings can be made; pastries chilled; tart cases blind-baked…

Simplify if needed

If you look at a menu of recipes and know you won't be able to cope with everything, don't. Buy dessert or ask a friend to make it. Replace one of the sides with a green salad. Buy good bread.

…AND YOUR STORECUPBOARD

Shopping is an awful lot easier if you can knowingly build up a good stock of the items you'll need. Olive oil, spices, vinegars, mustards and pickles are the sort of thing. If you happen to be passing, say, a Thai shop, and you know you'll need kaffir lime leaves at some point, buy them at the time and freeze them. Be an opportunist.

DELEGATE, BORROW AND GET HELP WITH ANYTHING YOU CAN

Taking care of all drinks on top of the food is a lot of work, so ask a knowledgeable friend to take the task on, in return for a good supper. Don't skimp on the quantities; you can return excess bottles of wine and beer. (But if you think you might, don't place them in ice buckets until you know you'll need them, or their labels will peel off.)

Set up early

Put up tables, if needed, and assemble chairs, cutlery, glasses and any decorations you want well in advance. Think of this as dressing a set for a play. Trying to lay the table attractively with two minutes to spare before a crowd arrives isn't exactly calming, so these are the ideal jobs to delegate to a willing friend a day or two beforehand.

DON'T BE AFRAID TO LET LARGE JOINTS OF MEAT REST,

tented with foil. They will not turn stone cold in 30 minutes.

EMBRACE YOUR INNER CONTROL FREAK:

budget, make lists, make more lists, be sure you have all the equipment needed and write a rough timetable for your prep and cooking. Wear a hands-free headset and a power suit if it helps.

ASK FAMILY AND FRIENDS FOR HELP WITH ADVANCE PREPARATION AND SETTING UP

Don't be precious, if you don't have enough, borrow chairs, cooking equipment, trestle tables, cutlery, glasses or crockery. A good, relaxed, party atmosphere is of far more importance than matching cutlery.

MAKE PUDDING IN ADVANCE

At least there will be something edible and ready to go; if all else fails, offer lots of wine and a lovely dessert. Rename it a pudding party.

MAKE USE OF THE INTERNET AND HOME DELIVERY

Ordering food online and by mail order has changed my life and a large order can mean you get a free delivery with some companies. Take full advantage.

ARTFULLY CONVINCE GUESTS TO SERVE THEMSELVES

With a bit of style and charm you can set up food (beautifully), on separate tables or on platters, ready for everyone to make up their own platefuls. Cunningly disguise this as a 'fun!' 'interactive!' activity and you won't have to assemble 20 perfect platefuls from a tiny kitchen. (See pages 18–21, 82 and 159 for some elegant examples of how to manage this.)

FINALLY, TRY TO STAY CALM

If everything goes wrong, it really isn't the end of the world. Make an emergency trip for bread and sausages or cheese and ham and have a glass of wine.

PINEAPPLE AND GINGER FIZZ

CHOOSE SWEET-SMELLING, YELLOW PINEAPPLES FOR THIS; it is important to be sure that they aren't sour or acidic. If the fruit is ripe, a spiky leaf should come away easily when tugged.

Infuriating to clean they may be, but if you have a juicer lurking at the back of a cupboard it will make short work of two sweet pineapples and a touch of ginger. A blender and a sieve will do the job too, so I've given directions for each.

If you don't like ginger, leave it out, or replace it with a handful of mint leaves to make tropical mojitos.

MAKES COCKTAILS UNTIL THE RUM RUNS OUT
PREP 15 MINUTES

FOR THE FRESH PINEAPPLE AND GINGER JUICE
2 large, fragrant and sweet pineapples
chubby thumb-sized piece of fresh root ginger

FOR EACH GLASS
50ml fresh pineapple and ginger juice
2-3 tbsp light rum, or more, to taste
½-1 tsp light brown sugar, to taste
crushed ice
soda water
edible flowers, lime or pineapple slices, to garnish

Top, tail and pare the tough skin from each pineapple. Only bother to core them if you are using a blender; a juicer will make short work of the woody centres. Cut the flesh into chunks. If you own a juicer, feed the pineapple in with the ginger. Pour into a large jug with 150ml iced water, mixing thoroughly.

If using a blender, chop the unpeeled ginger roughly. Working in three batches, whizz the pineapple and ginger together with 50ml water for each batch. Pour through a sieve into a large jug, discarding the pulp.

Either way, chill the juice until needed, for up to eight hours.

To make each cocktail, vigorously shake the pineapple and ginger juice, rum and sugar together with a few ice cubes. If you don't own a cocktail shaker – I certainly don't – a flask or large, lidded glass jar works perfectly. Strain into a tall glass filled with crushed ice, topping up with soda water to taste. Decorate with edible flowers, a lime slice or a fresh pineapple slice.

VEGETARIAN GARDEN BRUNCH FOR 8

EGGS EN COCOTTE WITH GOAT'S CHEESE, TARRAGON AND TOMATO | HERB FOUGASSE AND FIG AND MOZZARELLA PIZZAS
Toasted muesli bowls | SPRING JUICE BAR | LEMON AND ROSEMARY TART

If luck keeps the showers at bay, and you have the wherewithal, this feast of a menu is perfect to serve around a big, outdoor table. The difference in food bills between cooking a menu based on meat or fish, compared to a vegetarian spread, never ceases to amaze me. Reason enough, quite apart from the nourishing and celebratory recipes, to make this brunch. Whether you're cooking for a party of vegetarians or not, I wouldn't even mention the lack of carnivorous offerings; nobody will think to miss or notice anything. If the very idea of going meatless horrifies you – though I can't think why it should – drape parma ham over the cooked pizzas or top each baked egg cup with a shard of crisp bacon.

Getting in a panic before a supposedly relaxed brunch isn't particularly enjoyable, and there is a lot to do, so make the tart and the bread dough at your leisure, at least a day in advance. Ideal if you plan to eat on a Sunday. Likewise, get the muesli underway the night before and assemble your fruits and vegetables for juicing. You can even prepare the eggs the night before, up to the point of covering each cup with foil. On the day, cook the fougasse first, then let the eggs come up to room temperature for 20 minutes while you turn the oven down ready for them. Get somebody to help with the juices while you fire the oven back up, ready to finish off the pizzas to order.

A hearty brunch such as this will set you up for the whole day – I doubt anyone will want so much as a snack afterwards – so let everyone know they should arrive hungry. Stagger the food so as not to overwhelm, and to make things easier for you. I start serving the eggs around late morning or even midday on a lazy weekend day, and don't set any particular finishing time. The odd glass of champagne shouldn't be ruled out.

EGGS EN COCOTTE
WITH GOAT'S CHEESE, TARRAGON AND TOMATO

THESE HANDSOME CHAPS MANAGE TO BE BOTH ESPECIALLY SPRING-LIKE AND EXACTLY WHAT YOU'D WANT FOR BRUNCH. There is no need to be too thorough when deseeding the tomatoes, just get the bulk out. The seeds and surrounding jelly hold so much flavour that I rarely remove them, but unfortunately their presence would dilute the cream too much in this case. Besides, the bonny – and whole – cherry tomatoes release extra pops of sweetness to set the goat's cheese off beautifully.

Preheat the oven to 180°C/fan 160°C/350°F/gas mark 4. Lightly butter the insides of eight ovenproof cups or ramekins.

Cut a shallow cross in the base of all the medium tomatoes and place them in a bowl. Boil a kettle and pour the boiled water over the tomatoes to cover. Leave them for barely a minute – their skins should begin to lift and curl – then drain the water away and peel off the skins. Cut the tomatoes in half and scoop out the seeds with a teaspoon. Cut each half into two petals.

Divide the tomato petals, cherry tomatoes, cream, most of the tarragon and most of the goat's cheese between the cups or ramekins. Season well with salt and pepper. Crack an egg into each and finish with the remaining tarragon and goat's cheese. Sit the cups in a roasting tin and bake for 15–20 minutes, depending on whether you prefer a runny or a set yolk. Serve with teaspoons and Herb Fougasse soldiers (see page 34), for dipping.

SERVES 8
PREP 15 MINUTES
COOK 15 MINUTES

a little soft unsalted butter
6 ripe, medium tomatoes
large handful of mixed cherry
    tomatoes
300ml single cream
leaves from 3 sprigs of tarragon,
    chopped
150g soft goat's cheese log,
    sliced
8 very fresh, large eggs

HERB FOUGASSE AND FIG AND MOZZARELLA PIZZAS

ONE DOUGH, TWO IMPRESSIVE OUTCOMES... AND A KITCHEN THAT SMELLS LIKE HEAVEN. This is definitely one to make if you're selling your house and want to increase its appeal. Obviously, if you would like to make just the bread or just the pizzas, divide the dough quantities in half. Warming the flour and mixing bowl in a very low oven prior to mixing the sponge will really get the yeast going and adds a pleasingly sour flavour.

Assuming you will be making this for a late morning brunch and will be unwilling to get up at daybreak to start the dough, I suggest you make it the day before and allow it to rise slowly overnight.

I highly recommend a pizza stone to cook the pizzas; it will make a marked difference to the texture of the crust in a conventional oven and they are relatively inexpensive. Preheat the stone for as long as you can on a shelf near the top of the oven (I'd pop it in to preheat before cooking the eggs, just to give it a head start). Ease a flat baking sheet under the paper each proved pizza sits on, pull the oven shelf out and carefully slide each pizza from the baking sheet on to the hot stone, paper and all.

MAKES 2 LARGE PIZZAS AND 4 SMALL FOUGASSE LOAVES
PREP 40 MINUTES, PLUS 4½-6½ HOURS AND OVERNIGHT PROVING
COOK ABOUT 15 MINUTES FOR THE FOUGASSE; 10–12 MINUTES PER PIZZA

FOR THE DOUGH

- 600g strong white bread flour, plus more to dust
- 40g fresh yeast or 20g dried yeast (normal or fast acting)
- 2 tsp sea salt, plus more to scatter over before baking
- 75ml extra virgin olive oil, plus more to drizzle
- coarse semolina, to dust

Combine half the flour with the yeast and about 250ml hand-hot water in a large mixing bowl. Beat with a wooden spoon, or with the paddle attachment of a mixer, for three minutes or so. Cover the bowl with oiled cling film and set aside in a warm, not hot, place for three to four hours. I favour an airing cupboard or a barely-switched-on oven. Be careful, anything more than warm will kill the yeast and stop it rising. The sponge (for this is what you have made) will rise up and collapse back under its own weight during this time.

Add the remaining flour and 50ml more hand-hot water along with the salt and oil to make a very soft dough. Knead by hand on a lightly floured work surface, or in a mixer using a dough hook, for 10 minutes, until elastic and smooth. The mixture has a relatively loose consistency and is all the better for it, so don't be tempted to add too much extra flour. Keep persevering and the dough will become less sticky as you knead and develop the gluten in the flour.

Either cover the bowl with oiled cling film as before, or place the dough in a large food-grade bag, into which you have drizzled a little oil to prevent it from sticking. Force out the air and leave space for the dough to rise when sealing tightly. Place the bag or bowl in the refrigerator and leave to rise slowly overnight. Remove from the fridge at least 30 minutes before opening, to take the chill off.

CONT...

If you intend to cook the dough on the same day, a quicker rise will be called for: cover or bag it and return to the warm place to rise for an hour, or until doubled in size.

Punch the dough firmly to knock it back and divide it in half. Cover the half destined to make pizza bases – to stop it forming a crust – and set aside at room temperature while you make the fougasse.

To make the fougasse loaves, prepare a couple of large, flat baking sheets by oiling them (sparingly) and sprinkling lightly with semolina. Knead the basil, or herbs of your choice, into the dough and divide it into four pieces. Roll each out on a lightly floured surface to form a 3–4cm thick oval shape. Transfer two ovals to each baking sheet and, working one loaf at a time, cut a short vertical line up the centre. Now cut three short, diagonal slashes up each half, as if you were scoring the ribs in a simple leaf from near the central lines. Gently pull each cut apart with your hands, to form oblong holes in the dough. Cover the loaves with damp, clean tea towels or oiled cling film and set aside in a warm place to puff up for an hour. Meanwhile, preheat the oven to 230°C/fan 210°C/450°F/ gas mark 8. Drizzle each fougasse with a little olive oil, scatter with sea salt and bake for 15 minutes or so, until pale golden and risen. Cool on wire racks until just warm or at room temperature. Slice each loaf into soldiers at the table, ready to dip into the baked eggs.

To make the pizzas, have a couple of large, flat baking sheets (flat so that you can easily slide off the cooked pizzas) and two large squares of non-stick baking parchment at the ready.

Divide the pizza dough into two. Using a rolling pin and a little extra flour, roll and stretch each half out to form a rough circle. The dough should be very thin, about 5mm or thereabouts if you can.

Place a square of baking parchment on to each baking sheet and scatter lightly with semolina. Carefully transfer a pizza base on to each. Being careful to leave a border, cover the base with half the figs and mozzarella, finishing with a few basil leaves, a scattering of salt and a drizzle of olive oil. Leave to rise at room temperature for 20–30 minutes. Preheat the oven to 230°C/fan 210°C/450°F/gas mark 8 and position an oven rack near the top. Cook the pizzas one at a time, for about 10–12 minutes each, until the base is turning golden and the top is bubbling. If you have a pizza stone, preheat it as early as possible and slide each proved pizza on to it, as described in the recipe introduction.

Cut the cooked pizza into wedges – I find kitchen scissors the most effective way – scatter with a few more fresh basil leaves and serve hot, before quickly getting the next one into the oven.

FOR THE FOUGASSE
good handful of basil leaves
    or mixed soft herb leaves,
    chopped

FOR THE PIZZAS
6 plump figs, trimmed and sliced
3 balls of mozzarella, buffalo or
    cow, drained and roughly torn
good handful of basil leaves

TOASTED MUESLI BOWLS

TROPICAL FRUIT IS STILL FABULOUS AT THIS TIME OF YEAR, particularly the mangoes, of which the honeyed Indian Alphonso is most certainly king.

I favour using Rude Health's Morning Glory porridge mix in place of the rolled oats when I have a box in the house. It's a lovely blend of grains and seeds and makes a magnificent Bircher. You can use any hearty muesli mix too. If you, or anyone you want to make this for, is gluten intolerant, I have also had good results using purely quinoa flakes (from health food shops).

The toasting step ramps up the nuttiness of the oats nicely and lends them a firmer texture that will weather an overnight soaking. Do toast the nuts and seeds also; it makes a world of difference.

As with any Bircher muesli variation, you'll need to start this recipe the night before, but then most of the work will be done.

Toast the flaked almonds and seeds in a large frying pan, shaking it often until they begin to turn golden. Add the coconut for the last minute or so, it will toast fast so remove the pan from the heat before golden turns to burnt. Tip into a bowl and set aside. Return the pan to the heat and add a third or half of the oats or muesli, using a wooden spoon to keep everything moving. Keep cooking for about five minutes, until the oats turn a light brown and smell toasted. Tip into a large bowl and repeat once or twice more with the remaining oats.

Peel the mangoes with a swivel peeler and slice the fat cheeks from each, cutting either side of the flat stone. Take care as a peeled mango is rather slippery. Cut the remaining flesh from around the stone and dice it up. Combine with the grated apple, toasted oats or muesli mix, apple juice and half the toasted nut and seed mix, stirring well. Cover and chill overnight, or for a bare minimum of one hour if that's really all you have.

In the morning, divide the Bircher mixture between serving bowls and offer chopped tropical fruit, milk, yogurt and the remaining toasted nut and seed mixture to spoon or pour over. Each bowl can then be customised to taste. You may wish to finish with a drizzle of honey, but the fruit is likely to be sweet enough.

MAKES 8 GENEROUS BOWLFULS
PREP 20 MINUTES, PLUS OVERNIGHT SOAKING
COOK ABOUT 12-17 MINUTES, DEPENDING IN HOW MANY BATCHES YOU TOAST THE OATS

50g flaked almonds
50g pumpkin or sunflower seeds
2 tbsp unsweetened coconut flakes, or unsweetened desiccated coconut
400g rolled oats or muesli
3 large or 4 small mangoes
4 crunchy eating apples, cored and coarsely grated
700ml fresh apple and mango juice, or cloudy apple juice
peeled and chopped tropical fruits, such as banana, lychee, pineapple, kiwi and more mango, to serve
about 500ml cold milk, to serve
250g natural yogurt, to serve
mild honey, to serve (optional)

SPRING JUICE BAR

EACH MAKES 1 JUG
PREP 10–15 MINUTES PER JUICE

PURPLE

4 large beetroots, quartered

5 large carrots

4 pears, quartered

fat thumb-sized piece of fresh
    root ginger

squeeze of lemon juice, to finish

ROSE

10 large oranges, peeled

500g early strawberries, hulled

GREEN

6 apples, quartered

3 celery sticks

400g white grapes, removed
    from their stalks

2 handfuls of spinach leaves

handful of mint leaves

squeeze of lime, to finish

TO MAKE THE FRESH JUICES AS WRITTEN, YOU'LL NEED A JUICER. If you have one sulking at the back of the cupboard (I know. They are hellish to clean.) this is the time to dust it off. I buy cheap fruit and vegetables at my local market or greengrocer, going with whatever looks best, as it's usually better value than in most supermarkets.

Coerce a willing guest, family member or other half into making the juices for you when needed; they involve nothing more than feeding the prepared fruit and vegetables into the juicer, pressing down firmly with the plunger bit. Don't forget to put a large container by the collecting spout for the juice!

If you don't own a juicer and can't borrow one, just buy several different, ready-made, fresh juices and chill them down thoroughly. Combine on the day to make your own mixtures. Or squeeze a couple of jugs of orange juice from fresh oranges.

The following are merely suggestions. Each will fill one jug, or about four glasses. Do try other combinations, depending on what's abundant and in season.

Juice each combination in your machine. Stir each juice well before finishing with the citrus (in the case of the purple and green varieties), then pouring them into large jugs with a little ice. Serve straight away, when the vitamins and minerals are at their most plentiful and beneficial.

Group the juices at one end of the table, encouraging your guests to help themselves before they sit down to eat. Provide spoons or muddlers to stir each glass again before drinking; freshly made juices will naturally separate slightly on sitting.

Hedgerow Foraging

Blooming springtime has much to offer for the amateur to go a-foraging. No trespassing, mind. My handsome Opinel folding knife serves very well as a collecting tool. I've detailed a small selection of well-known and easily recognised plants below. One final nag: if you're not absolutely sure what you're picking, leave well alone and cook some pasta instead.

A FEW GEMS TO GET ACQUAINTED WITH:

ELDERFLOWERS

Flat and frothy heads of tiny white blossom adorn bushy, (usually) low-growing elderflower trees in late spring and early summer. They are plentiful in town and country throughout the UK. Look for them in hedgerows and along the edge of woodland; you will be able to detect the blooms' musky perfume from some distance.

Use the flower heads straight away, shaken free of any tiny insects, to make an intense elderflower cordial for drinks, jellies and sorbets. Or infuse barely-scalded cream with fresh elderflowers, strain and use to make possets, pannacottas, mousses, custards and ice creams. Coated in a light batter and fried, the heads make a delightful, airy fritter. I adore these, dusted with icing sugar, as a piping-hot accompaniment to homemade elderflower ice cream.

WILD GARLIC

In rural Sussex, where I'm from, there is much shaking of heads at London folk paying for wild garlic leaves by the box or bag. Why would you when they grow so freely below hedges, in damp woodlands and along river banks? Follow your nose; wild garlic gently reeks of... garlic. Unsurprisingly. Look for elegant and pointed, grey-green and shiny leaves, rather like tulip leaves in appearance. The white flower heads bob about on vertical stems and resemble large chive flowers. Cut from near the base, leaving each plant with enough leaves to keep growing, and store in the fridge for a few days, loosely wrapped in damp newspaper. Use both leaves and flowers in stir-fries and sauces and, when very young, in salads. Wild garlic pesto – made by pounding the leaves, pine nuts, parmesan and olive oil together – is a joy with pasta and in paninis. Or stuff chicken breasts with soft cheese and the chopped leaves then wrap in larger leaves, followed by a layer of parma ham. Roast until cooked through.

PRIMROSE FLOWERS AND VIOLETS

Go carefully when gathering blossoms from primroses and their ilk... they are a legally protected flower in the wild so, unless you grew them yourself or are in a private garden with permission from the owner, you definitely shouldn't be taking them. If you are lucky enough to have some in your garden, however, a few of the sweet flowers make a beautiful addition to spring salads. If it appeals, both primroses and violets can be crystallised – coat in turn with egg white and caster sugar, then dry – ready to decorate cakes and desserts.

DANDELION LEAVES

Everybody should be able to recognise the ubiquitous and nutrituous dandelion. It must be a rare person who didn't try to tell the time by blowing at a fluffy, round seed head when they were a kid. Speaking of which, I used to detest the plants' bitterness but, as an adult, a few of the young leaves in a mixed salad now appeals greatly. Gather the dark green leaves, which look rather like rocket leaves, from grassland and hedgerows, cutting from near the base and being sure to wash well before use. The entire plant is edible and the root can be sliced and stir-fried, or sautéed. You could also add the bright yellow and densely petalled flowers to green salads to pretty them up.

CHICKWEED

Chickweed grows vigorously and low to the ground, in a sprawling fashion. The diminutive, spade-shaped leaves adorn slender stems with five-petalled, white, daisy-like flowers at the top. Look out for it in flowerbeds, hedgerows and at the edge of woodlands. Snap a stem as a test and, if a milky (rather than clear) sap runs out, it is not chickweed and you shouldn't eat it.

Omelettes and frittatas, quiches and tarts, pastas, risottos, soups, stir-fries, sandwiches and salads will all benefit from chickweed's mildly herby and fresh flavour, not unlike sweetcorn when raw, not to mention its high vitamin C content. It will wilt down quickly, however, so only add at the very last minute if you intend to cook it.

MORELS

Spring mushrooms don't get as much press as their autumn cousins but study any sparsely covered ground, as you walk through deciduous woodland, and you might luck out with clusters of morels. The highly-domed and dark grey or brown mushroom caps are intricately folded; rather like the outside of a human brain! The stalks are low and creamy-white. Morels really are easy to spot and difficult to confuse. Once you get used to the woody surroundings, you might even be able to smell their spores in the air, leading you to more mushrooms downwind of the scent.

The best time to hunt is about three days after rainfall and no later than 11am. Take a paper bag to collect your wares and avoid looking just after, or during, frosts... you won't find any then. When you get home, brush away any dirt and leaves rather than washing the morels, then cook as soon as possible. Foaming butter, chopped

garlic and sourdough toast never went amiss where mushrooms are concerned.

Another note: a compound in morels reacts with alcohol to cause mild stomach upsets, so don't cook them with much wine and don't drink much with them. Half a glass is the limit, I'm afraid. If in the slightest doubt, leave wild mushrooms well alone. Do err on the side of caution, please.

STINGING NETTLES

Rubber gloves mandatory...

Identification should be relatively easy with this one. If the leaves and stalks sting, the plant stands at 50cm to two metres tall, the tiny flowers are green or brownish and the leaves are heart-shaped and raggedy, you have a stinging nettle. Go for the new growth at the top, first snipping off the bitter top pair of leaves, which are pale in colour.

Like spinach, it takes a lot of nettle to produce any bulk because they shrink so much. The best thing to make is a smooth nettle and potato soup, but a barely wilted and buttery pasta or gnocchi sauce is also a good idea. Risottos work well, or use a few leaves to make a tea said to help with water retention and high blood pressure.

If this subject tickles your fancy and you want to take it further, get hold of a foraging guide with colour reference pictures. Not only will you widen your horizons and have an excuse to spend the day outside, you'll be much less likely to confuse non-edibles with edibles...

LEMON AND ROSEMARY TART

SERVES 8-12
PREP 40 MINUTES, PLUS
   CHILLING
COOK 45 MINUTES

FOR THE PASTRY

350g plain flour
½ tsp salt
90g icing sugar, sifted
175g unsalted butter, chilled
   and diced
2 tbsp finely chopped rosemary
   leaves
3 egg yolks, from chilled eggs

FOR THE FILLING

finely grated zest and juice of 5
   unwaxed lemons
215g caster sugar
4 eggs, plus 6 egg yolks
2 sprigs of rosemary
200g unsalted butter, cubed

1 tbsp icing sugar
crème fraîche or whipped cream,
   to serve (optional)

DURING UNIVERSITY HOLIDAYS, I MADE THE RIVER CAFÉ'S LEMON TART WITH ALARMING REGULARITY at the Griffin Inn in Sussex. I could probably make the filling in my sleep!

The pure lemon is, of course, pretty perfect, but in my version a judicious amount of rosemary marries beautifully with the citrus. So much so that I always make it this way now.

Use a 23cm diameter round tart tin if you don't have a 20x30cm rectangular one. You'll need to make this the day before to let it firm up. I dispense with caramelising a dusting of icing sugar across the surface, but don't let that stop you if you're handy with a blowtorch.

Start with the pastry. Pulse the flour, salt and sugar in a food processor a couple of times to aerate it. Add the butter and pulse just until the mixture resembles breadcrumbs, being careful not to overwork or it will be tough. Sprinkle the rosemary over and add the egg yolks. Pulse again, until the pastry starts to clump together. Tip on to a work surface and knead lightly, just until smooth. Form into a fat cylinder and wrap in clingfilm. Chill for at least an hour.

Once the pastry has chilled, preheat the oven to 180°C/fan 160°C/350°F/gas mark 4. Slice the cylinder into discs, each no thinner than a pound coin. Lay these discs side-by-side over the base and sides of a fluted 20x30cm rectangular tart tin, with a removable base. Press the pastry out with your fingertips to form a uniform lining, leaving the edges untrimmed and sitting proud of the tin. Prick the base lightly with a fork a few times.

Line with a large rectangle of non-stick baking parchment and fill with ceramic baking beans, dried pulses or uncooked rice. Bake for 15 minutes, until the base no longer looks raw, then remove the paper and beans or rice and continue to cook for five to 10 minutes more until the pastry is a pale biscuit colour and looks 'sandy' and dry. Remove from the oven and, once cool enough, use a sharp knife to trim the edges flush with the tin, brushing the trimmings away. Gingerly press the removable base and work a knife tip into any corners that stick, just until the pastry lifts away. If the pastry welds itself to the tin at this stage, there will be trouble when you come to release it later. Leave to cool completely in the tin.

To make the filling, whisk the lemon zest and juice, sugar, eggs, egg yolks and sprigs of rosemary together in a large saucepan until amalgamated. Don't worry if the rosemary gets caught up in the whisk, it will still be releasing its oils and doing its work.

Set over a very low heat and whisk slowly as you add half the butter. Don't stop whisking or let the heat get too high or you'll have scrambled eggs. Once the first lot of butter has been incorporated, add the second, bit by bit. Keep whisking and heating gently until the mixture thickens enough to leave a trail behind the whisk. Remove from the heat and pour through a sieve into a large jug.

Sit the jug in a sink part-filled with cold water. Keep whisking intermittently to prevent a skin forming, until the curd has cooled to body temperature (close your eyes and prod with a clean finger; you shouldn't detect much of a temperature difference). Drape cling film directly over the surface and leave to cool to room temperature. (A note for nervous cooks: you can make the filling in a heatproof bowl over gently simmering water. It will take longer but is safer.) Pour the filling into the tart case and smooth the top. Chill for at least six hours or overnight to set.

Slice into rectangles and dust with icing sugar just before serving. Crème fraîche or whipped cream will cut through the lemon.

HOLIDAY WEEKEND AWAY FOR 8

BRUNCH: | **BANANA, DATE AND MAPLE THICKIE** | *Merguez sausages, spiced potatoes and eggs* | **LUNCH:** | PORCHETTA STUFFED WITH FARRO, WITH FARRO AND GREEN BEAN SALAD | **EARLY BEETS IN PARCELS** | APRICOT AND FIRST RASPBERRY LATTICE TART | **FROZEN YOGURT** *Supper:* | **GALETTES DE BLE NOIR** KOHLRABI SALAD

A late spring public holiday, when the sun feels truly warm for the first time, is one of life's ultimate pleasures. That reassuring moment arrives when the landscape bursts into summer again, leaving short, dark days far behind. There is an element of risk involved, for the weather might turn on you, sulking in damp clouds, but when the days set fair and fairer still and the nights retain a jab of chill, this can be the very best time to holiday close to home.

You might be cooking in your own home, in which case the following will mercifully not apply. Unless you are housed in luxury and grandeur, cooking in a holiday home can be... a challenge, even with a group of you to muck in. It is likely that you will not have a particularly well-equipped kitchen; the oven might be archaic. So if you know you will be cooking a tart or a particular cake, take the tin with you; they are usually light to transport. Less portable but still important is a good, large frying pan and a couple of sharp kitchen knives (I have never stayed in a rented house boasting sharp knives). Wrap the blades in several tea towels and tie in place with string. A sharp swivel peeler for vegetables is invaluable and I will confess to taking my small, light mandolin along to slice salad vegetables in no time. If you don't know if the kitchen has a blender, take a hand-held stick blender along, they are very light. Plan to cook one big lunch and one casual supper. Take the ingredients and plenty of milk and juices with you. Beyond that, my advice is this: don't get bogged down in shopping, cooking and clearing up for the entire weekend. There will be pubs serving food, chip shops, or restaurants. Have a nose around for a few ideas before you go. Cook a few lovely things but, otherwise, eat leftovers and cheese and crackers; get outside, explore, have fun.

ESSENTIAL KIT
for weekends away

A holiday home will have the basics in place. If you're lucky or have splashed out, the kitchen might be a palace, replete with every gadget you could ever wish for. Check with the owners first to avoid doubling up, but here are a few useful extras to pack up in a box...

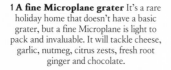

1 A fine Microplane grater It's a rare holiday home that doesn't have a basic grater, but a fine Microplane is light to pack and invaluable. It will tackle cheese, garlic, nutmeg, citrus zests, fresh root ginger and chocolate.

2 A measuring jug Often elusive, this is pretty essential for measuring liquids if you plan on doing any baking.

3 Frying pan A really good-quality, non-stick frying pan – as large as possible – will knock any battered old holiday home pan for six. Use it as a wok and griddle for crêpes, as well as for fry-ups.

4 A balloon whisk For airy batters, egg whites and smooth sauces.

5 A hand-held blender Instead of an upright, for smoothies, soups and the like; a basic hand-held is surprisingly light.

6 A sharp cook's knife Just one, large and sharp, to replace the inevitably blunt selection on offer. Wrap the blade in layers of sturdy tea towels and tie in place to transport safely. The tea towels will come in useful too.

7 Plastic food bags, cling film, foil and non-stick baking parchment Self-explanatory and invaluable.

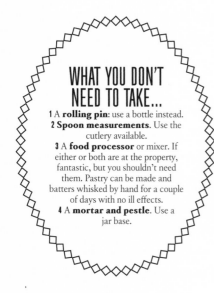

WHAT YOU DON'T NEED TO TAKE...
1 A **rolling pin**: use a bottle instead.
2 Spoon measurements. Use the cutlery available.
3 A **food processor** or mixer. If either or both are at the property, fantastic, but you shouldn't need them. Pastry can be made and batters whisked by hand for a couple of days with no ill effects.
4 A **mortar and pestle**. Use a jar base.

8 A sharp vegetable peeler Of the swivel or Y variety. For peeling vegetables and fruit, or paring and shredding for salads.

9 A small mandolin My cheap Japanese mandolin is invaluable for thinly slicing crunchy vegetables and firm fruits more quickly and uniformly than knives could.

10 Scales A light set of electronic scales for baking; far more accurate than a cheap pair of mechanical scales.

11 Cake tins and pie dishes If you plan on baking anything, take the right tin along. Fudging a cake recipe with the wrong-sized tin in an unfamiliar oven might end in tears...

BRUNCH
BANANA, DATE AND MAPLE THICKIE

TO CRUSH ICE CUBES, WRAP THEM IN A TEA TOWEL AND BASH energetically with a rolling pin. Thwacking the rolled-up tea towel on a tiled surface or floor also does the job. Both methods should rid you of any latent tension.

Blitz everything together in a blender. Wrap a tea towel over the lid and hold it firmly as you blend, this should stop any potential overflow getting out of hand. Failing this, use a hand-held stick blender and a deep bowl, covering it with a tea towel to prevent splash-back.

Taste and add a little more maple syrup if you want, but I doubt you'll think it necessary.

SERVES 4, BUT EASILY DOUBLED
PREP 10 MINUTES

3 large, ripe bananas
handful of Medjool dates, stoned
3 tbsp rolled oats
2 tbsp maple syrup, or to taste
450ml natural yogurt
300ml whole milk
about 12 ice cubes, crushed

AND A VERY FEW USEFUL STORECUPBOARD ESSENTIALS.
Take these as well as any ingredients you'll need for specific recipes.
1 A good **olive oil** that will double up for both cooking and salad dressings.
2 A good **balsamic vinegar** for dressings.
3 **Plain flour** and **baking powder** for impromptu, fluffy breakfast pancakes.
4 **Nuts and seeds** for cereal and porridge, to use in baking, or to be toasted and scattered in salads.
5 Sea **salt** and black **peppercorns**.
6 **Herbs** such as rosemary, bay, sage and thyme, though these can be found about the place if you're lucky and it has a garden.

BRUNCH
MERGUEZ SAUSAGES, SPICED POTATOES AND EGGS

SERVES 8
PREP 20 MINUTES
COOK ABOUT 1 HOUR

FOR THE SPICE MIX

3 tbsp cumin seeds
3 tbsp coriander seeds
1 tbsp black peppercorns
1 cinnamon stick
½ tsp yellow or black mustard
    seeds
1 tsp dried chilli flakes
1 tsp turmeric
1 tbsp smoked paprika
½ tsp freshly ground nutmeg

FOR THE BRUNCH ITSELF

600g new potatoes, halved
    if large
16 merguez sausages (the
    thinner sort)
5 tbsp olive oil
2 large onions, halved and sliced
2 red peppers, deseeded and cut
    into strips
5 tomatoes, each cut into six
100g spinach, washed and
    drained well
8 very, very fresh eggs (optional)
small handful of chopped parsley
a little smoked paprika (optional)
harissa paste, to serve (optional)

BLENDING SMALL BATCHES OF SPICES AT HOME allows you subtly to adjust the balance until it suits your taste. Cloves, allspice, cayenne or saffron (all in judicious amounts), or fennel seeds, mace or ginger, would be worthwhile additions to the basic mix as written. If you start by buying the whole spices from a good Asian shop with a fast turnover, then toast and grind, the results will knock most bought blends for six. Not to mention the convenience of using one ready-to-go jar, as opposed to rootling around in the back of the cupboard for 10 different spices halfway through a recipe (just me?).

Make your spice mix a few days beforehand and keep in a lidded jar for up to three months. Note its name and use-by date on a label. You won't have trouble using it up: dust over fish, chicken or vegetables before roasting, stir into olive oil to finish a lentil soup, or spoon on to softened onions and garlic at the start of a tagine.

You could quite easily use a bought spice mix for this recipe instead of making your own. It needs to match the flavours of the sausages and complement the vegetables, so try a ras el hanout, translated as 'top of the shop'. Each spice merchant supposedly makes his own secret North African blend with his very best spices, hence the name.

Here, crisp, spiced potatoes accompany merguez sausages, stained with smoked paprika, and a panful of colourful vegetables. To finish it all off, top with a poached (or fried, if you prefer) egg and a little chopped parsley. Breakfast or brunch fodder for champions.

Start by making your spice mix. Toast the spices, except for the turmeric, paprika and nutmeg, gently in a dry frying pan, stirring them to toast evenly. Remove from the heat when they look slightly darker – but not burnt – and smell fragrant. Add the turmeric, paprika and nutmeg and either pound everything together in a mortar and pestle, or grind in a spice mill or a small coffee grinder (permanently designated to grinding spices, rather than beans, for the sake of your morning coffee). Store in a lidded jar, label and use within three months.

When you are ready to cook brunch, preheat the oven to 220°C/fan 200°C/425°F/gas mark 7.

Par-boil the potatoes in plenty of simmering water and a pinch of

CONT...

salt for 15 minutes or so, until just tender to the point of a knife. Drain in a colander.

Meanwhile, quickly brown the sausages with 2 tbsp of the oil, in two batches if necessary, in a large frying pan set over a high heat. Once seared, remove to a roasting tin with a slotted spoon, leaving the paprika-stained oil in the pan.

Add the potatoes to the sausages in their roasting tin, with the remaining oil. Tumble around to coat everything in oil, then scatter with 1½ tbsp of the spice mix. Roast for 15–20 minutes, until the potatoes are turning golden. Turn the oven off with the tin still inside and leave the door ajar. Add a stack of plates to warm them up.

Get a deep frying pan, full of water, coming up to the boil if you intend on poaching eggs.

Throw the onions and peppers into the frying pan with the oil from the sausages and 1 tsp of spice mix. Fry over a medium heat, stirring often, for about 10 minutes, until all is softened and beginning to brown. Now add the tomatoes and cook for a further 10 minutes, stirring and adding a splash of water if anything sticks. Fold in the spinach and remove from the heat. Season well and keep warm.

When the poached egg water is simmering gently – that's lots of gentle bubbles but no violent boiling – submerge the eggs, whole and in their shells, beneath the water for 20 seconds. Remove with a slotted spoon. One-by-one, carefully crack each egg into a small cup. Hold the cup as near to the water's surface as possible and gently slide the egg in, causing as little disturbance as possible. Repeat with the other eggs. Leave to cook at this very gentle simmer for three to four minutes, until the whites are set but the yolks are still liquid. You may need gently to encourage them to lift off the bottom if they sink downwards. Use a slotted spoon to remove the eggs to a plate, first allowing any excess water to drain away.

Serve a small pile of potatoes and a couple of sausages with a good spoonful of the vegetable mixture. Top each warmed plateful with an egg and a scattering of parsley. You could add a rust-red dusting of smoked paprika, if you have some handy. Offer harissa on the side for those who like the heat.

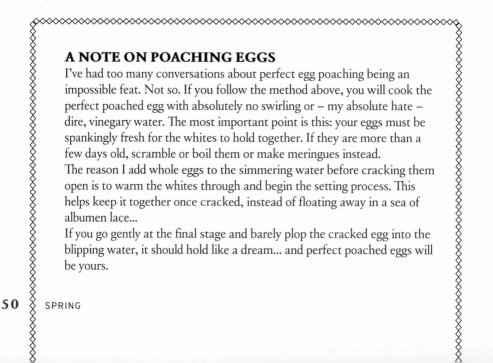

A NOTE ON POACHING EGGS

I've had too many conversations about perfect egg poaching being an impossible feat. Not so. If you follow the method above, you will cook the perfect poached egg with absolutely no swirling or – my absolute hate – dire, vinegary water. The most important point is this: your eggs must be spankingly fresh for the whites to hold together. If they are more than a few days old, scramble or boil them or make meringues instead.

The reason I add whole eggs to the simmering water before cracking them open is to warm the whites through and begin the setting process. This helps keep it together once cracked, instead of floating away in a sea of albumen lace...

If you go gently at the final stage and barely plop the cracked egg into the blipping water, it should hold like a dream... and perfect poached eggs will be yours.

LUNCH
EARLY BEETS IN PARCELS

THIS IS HARDLY A FORMAL RECIPE. THINK OF IT AS A SUGGESTION and adjust the quantities to your taste, adding more or no garlic, a different herb, a sweet sherry vinegar...

Any available beetroots should be small and tender this early in the season. Chop any larger ones into wedges. You'll also need baking parchment and kitchen string, or foil, for wrapping.

Preheat the oven to 190°C/fan 170°C/375°F/gas mark 5. Slice smaller beetroots in half, or quarter if large.

Cut out eight squares of foil or baking parchment; each needs to be about 20cm square. Scrunch the paper up a little to stop liquid running straight out of it and, in the centre of each square, sit a pile of beetroots, a bruised garlic clove, a couple of sprigs of thyme, a scattering of salt and pepper, a splash of balsamic and the same of olive oil.

Fold and wrap the excess paper in, as if you were wrapping a present. Tie in place with kitchen string. If you use foil, no string will be needed, you can just crush the edges into place.

Bake for one hour, until the beets are glazed, tender and concentrated in flavour. Take the parcels to the table and let everybody unwrap their own.

SERVES 8 AS A SIDE DISH
PREP 20 MINUTES
COOK 1 HOUR

12-16 young multicoloured
   beetroots, scrubbed, topped
   and tailed
8 fat garlic cloves, bruised, but
   left whole and in their skins
handful of sprigs of thyme
good balsamic vinegar
extra virgin olive oil

LUNCH
PORCHETTA STUFFED WITH FARRO

PORCHETTA, YES, BUT DONE MY WAY, with a garlic-scented farro stuffing that intensifies as the pork roasts to tenderness. The extra grain cooked makes the base for a warm salad to accompany the joint.

You can find newly trendy farro in delis with a good stock of Italian ingredients, or in health food shops. Substitute with spelt or barley, which have similar nutty tones but slightly less texture once cooked.

Toast the pine nuts in a dry frying pan, shaking often until golden. Combine the garlic, rosemary and sage in a bowl and set aside.

In a large casserole or saucepan, soften the onions in the olive oil for 10 minutes, until colouring at the edges. Add half the chopped garlic and herb mixture and cook for a few seconds, then stir in the farro and stock. Bring to the boil, cover and simmer, lid askew, for 30 minutes, or until the liquid has been absorbed and the grains are tender, but not insipidly so. Stir in the pine nuts and cool slightly.

Meanwhile, preheat your oven to its highest setting. To make it easier to tie the pork after stuffing it, cut five lengths of kitchen string – each about 40cm if you're measuring – and lay them out in parallel, each evenly spaced below the other. Lay the pork on top, skin-side down. Make a few more shallow cuts in the flesh to increase its surface area, then smear the remaining garlic and herbs all over with plenty of salt and pepper. Spoon a scant quarter of the farro down the middle then bring the sides up around it and roll as tightly as you can. Tie the string tightly around to keep the shape.

Now anoint the surface with about 2 tbsp olive oil and rub liberally with salt to help the skin crisp as it roasts. Lay the celery, carrot and shallots in a sturdy roasting tin, sit the pork on top and add the wine with 300ml water. Slide into the centre of the oven and immediately reduce the heat to 180°C/fan 160°C/350°F/gas mark 4. Roast for 3–3½ hours, until deeply golden, crisp and beginning to bubble.

Rest the pork in the tin for a few minutes. Snip through the string and carve into slices; you might find it easier to remove the crisp skin in one go first. Place the tin over a low heat, scraping to remove any good caramelised bits and adding a dash more water to make a light gravy. Strain into a jug. Serve the pork with the Farro and Green Bean Salad (see page 54) and the warm pan juices.

SERVES 8
PREP 30 MINUTES
COOK 3¾–4¼ HOURS

FOR THE FARRO STUFFING (WITH LEFTOVER FOR THE SALAD, SEE PAGE 54)
100g pine nuts
4 fat garlic cloves, finely chopped
leaves from 4 sprigs of rosemary, chopped
6 large sage leaves, chopped
2 large red onions, chopped
3 tbsp olive oil, plus more for the crackling
500g farro or spelt
920ml light vegetable stock or water

FOR THE PORK
3kg pork shoulder, boned, butterflied and skin scored
2 celery sticks, roughly chopped
1 carrot, roughly chopped
2 banana shallots, halved, or 1 onion, sliced (no need to peel)
250ml white wine

LUNCH
FARRO AND GREEN BEAN SALAD

SERVES 8 GENEROUSLY
PREP 20 MINUTES
COOK 5 MINUTES

FOR THE DRESSING
5 tbsp extra virgin olive oil, or
    to taste
2 tbsp red wine vinegar, or
    to taste
pinch of sugar, or to taste

FOR THE SALAD
cooked farro base from
    Porchetta Stuffed with Farro
    (see page 53)
500g green beans, topped
200g young carrots, scrubbed,
    sliced only if larger than a
    little finger
2 handfuls of mixed summer
    herbs, finely chopped
200g ricotta salata, roughly
    crumbled

THIS WILL MAKE A LOVELY ACCOMPANIMENT TO THE PORK but, if you have any vegetarians in your party, a warm salad makes an excellent main course to compensate for the lack of pork and will still be very good cold the following day. I've assumed you'll be making both but that is rather arrogant of me so, if you'd like to rebel and make the salad without making the pork, follow the instructions in the Porchetta Stuffed with Farro recipe (see page 53) with the odd adjustment. Soften the onions but add slightly less of the chopped garlic and herbs. Use only 400g farro or spelt and 800ml stock or water, then simmer until cooked as in the main recipe. Add the toasted pine nuts once cooked.

If you can't get ricotta salata, use a firm but fresh-tasting, salty cheese; try a young pecorino or even a crumbled Wensleydale or Lancashire. For the mixed herbs, I used snipped chives and chive flowers, with mint, basil and chervil, but any soft spring herbs you like will be lovely here; the key is bounty so use a free hand.

Combine the dressing ingredients with salt and pepper. Taste and adjust with more oil, vinegar or sugar until it tastes good to you.

If the cooked farro is cold, cover and warm through in a low oven.

Steam the beans and carrots over boiling water for about four minutes, until just tender. Add to the farro with the herbs, stir briefly, then douse with the dressing. Fold through the ricotta. Taste and add more seasoning if needed. Serve warm.

Wild Swimming

What better after a weekend walk and a picnic than to happen upon some halcyon pond, pool, beach or looping river bend to laze about in? The best are tranquil spots, away from the madding crowds, but you might have to work hard at discovering them. Keep the splashing to a minimum and you're likely to see all sorts of wildlife, both above and below the water.

PONDS AND SMALL LAKES

Are invariably warmer than the sea; in the later days of a good summer, it's not unusual for the water temperature to reach a balmy 20°C. At other times of the year – and for sea swimming – a wetsuit might be an idea.

WATERFALL AND PLUNGE POOLS

Fed by a waterfall or, in less-spectacular cases, a stream, plunge pools are usually icy-cool and, hopefully, deep enough to dive into (it is ALWAYS absolutely essential to check this before jumping in!).

Enormous coastal rock pools, left for a few hours at low tide, also make ideal salt-water swimming pools and there will be a great deal to look at below the surface and in surrounding, smaller, rock pools.

COASTLINES

For the brave swimmer, undeterred by cold, the UK is blessed with a plethora of sandy beaches, rocky outcrops, secret bays, islands, arches and caves to discover. Take a snorkel; you'll be amazed at what you can see. Get to know the stretch of coastline you're exploring, including the tide times and any areas with high currents or unsuitable ground that should be avoided.

SLOW-MOVING RIVERS

Meandering rivers, housing bends and loops with very little current, often provide the perfect conditions for a swim. The water will be cold where the sun's rays can't reach, so float on the surface or prepare for cold legs!

SAFETY ADVICE

Getting overly 'health and safety' takes away from the pleasure of wild swimming so, assuming you are a strong swimmer, don't trespass, and use your common sense. However, there are a few rules to stick to, especially when venturing into a location you don't know well:

Never swim where fishermen are. Their potential wrath at the disturbance should be enough to put you off, but a barbed hook through the eye would be so much worse.

When assessing a river for swimming potential, look for fords and firm, sloping banks so that you can climb out easily. Wear shoes to protect your feet and ease in slowly, making sure you're happy with the depth.

If you are worried about the cleanliness of the water, contact your local environment agency beforehand for information.

Our coastline houses a veritable treasure chest of secluded bays and beaches, but the ocean can be brutal so play it safe and always leave yourself a generous amount of leeway. Fishermen and wise locals should know what's what, so ask them about tides, incoming weather and known danger spots. Be aware if rising tides could strand you on a section of beach or rock.

3 of my favourite WILD SWIMMING SPOTS

TREYARNON BAY beach on the north coast of Cornwall reveals spectacular – and very large – rock pools at low tide. They are perfect for swimming and paddling, though wetsuit boots or jelly shoes with a good grip are recommended to protect soft feet from the rocks and any sharp underwater creatures.

The stunning INGRAM VALLEY houses the River Breamish and runs through Northumberland National Park. The river itself is suitable for a paddle and a splash-about in warm weather, but follow the road to the end of the valley and walk up the marked path for a couple of miles, to reach Linhope Spout, a particularly beautiful waterfall with a plunge pool below for swimming in.

Local to my family home is THE ANCHOR INN, just outside Barcombe in East Sussex. From there, it's well known that you can hire rowing boats to amble along the Ouse towards a pretty weir. Most give up and turn around before they get to the end, but it's worth the inevitable arm ache for a secluded dip. There are plenty of rope swings and swim-worthy river bends to amuse on a shorter trip though. Just be prepared to dodge shrieking, dive-bombing teenagers in high summer (I was one of them not so long ago...).

LUNCH
APRICOT AND FIRST RASPBERRY LATTICE TART

SERVES 8, WITH ICE CREAM
PREP 30 MINUTES, PLUS
   CHILLING TIME
COOK 1 HOUR

a little plain flour, for rolling
500g shortcrust pastry (slightly
   sweetened, ideally)
3 tbsp ground almonds
4 tbsp brown sugar
7 ripe apricots, halved and
   stoned
200g raspberries
whole milk, to glaze
2 tbsp demerara sugar (optional)

A PUDDING TO CELEBRATE THOSE TENTATIVE EARLY RASPBERRIES. If none are to be found, buy them frozen instead and defrost before using.

The filling isn't overly saccharine, so this rustic, juicy mix benefits from a good and short shortcrust pastry recipe with a touch of sweetness. You might want to halve the pastry component for the Chicken and Wild Mushroom Pies (see page 124), stirring in 2 tbsp icing sugar before adding the water. An all-butter bought pastry would do perfectly well, too.

First dusting with a very little flour, roll the pastry out into a large circle, the thickness of a two-pound coin. Line a 20cm pie dish, being careful not to stretch the pastry or it will shrink back on cooking. Trim the edges with scissors, leaving a good 1cm overhang. Chill for at least 30 minutes or up to a few hours. Preheat the oven to 180°C/fan 160°C/350°F/gas mark 4.

Now trim the excess pastry flush with the tin, using a sharp knife. Scatter the base with the ground almonds and about 1 tbsp of the brown sugar. Lay the apricots on top, cut-sides up, and scatter with half the remaining brown sugar. Sprinkle the raspberries on and around, finishing with the last of the brown sugar.

Re-roll the remaining pastry and cut into strips of about 25cm. Lay these across the top in a lattice pattern, sticking them into place with a drop of milk. Brush the lattice with milk and, if you like, dredge with demerara sugar to create a crunchy sugar top.

Bake for about one hour, covering loosely with foil if the pastry lattice browns too quickly. Serve warm, straight from the tin with the frozen yogurt, if you have made it. Otherwise, cream, crème fraîche or vanilla ice cream would make lovely substitutes.

FROZEN YOGURT

IF YOU HAVE AN ICE CREAM MACHINE, you can get away with using a good, whole milk yogurt but, if you make this by hand (almost certainly the case in a holiday house), the density of a full-fat Greek yogurt is essential for a really creamy result.

Stir the yogurt, sugar, lemon juice and vanilla until the sugar dissolves. Chill in the freezer for an hour. If you have one, freeze in an ice cream maker according to the manufacturer's instructions.

All is not lost, however, if you need to make this by hand. Freeze the chilled mixture in a sturdy, shallow container for one hour, then whisk vigorously with a balloon whisk to break up and mix in any ice crystals at the edges. Return to the freezer for 30 minutes, then whisk again, repeating this every half hour for another two hours. Leave to firm up in the freezer for an hour or two. This is best soon after making but will keep, covered, for a couple of weeks. In the latter case, soften in the refrigerator until scoopable before serving.

SERVES 8 AS AN ACCOMPANIMENT
PREP 10 MINUTES, PLUS 1 HOUR CHILLING
FREEZE 20–30 MINUTES IN AN ICE CREAM MACHINE; ABOUT 3½ HOURS BY HAND.

700g thick, Greek-style yogurt (not reduced fat), chilled
120g caster sugar
2 tsp lemon juice
½ vanilla pod, seeds scraped out, or 1 tsp vanilla extract

SUPPER
GALETTES DE BLÉ NOIR

SUCH A LYRICAL NAME WHEN COMPARED TO THEIR ENGLISH TRANSLATION: buckwheat crêpes, Breton-style. This batter is a dream for making ahead as it needs to settle and swell overnight before making the crêpes. Use the largest frying pan or crêpe pan you can get your hands on. A cast-iron, flat griddle will produce the ultimate in galettes, but improvising is just fine. This filling is traditional and simple; lovely for brunch or lunch as well as an early supper. Using egg yolks only is a solution to the egg white taking too long to cook and ruining the timings. A poached or fried egg, added before folding the crêpe, would solve that problem. Distinctive, toasty buckwheat is found in blinis, so it follows that smoked salmon, crème fraîche or cream cheese and dill is welcome in a crisp-edged galette. Or try sautéed leeks, ham and gruyère or just ham and gruyère with no egg yolk; buttered spinach, nutmeg and ricotta; buttered spinach and gruyère; jam and butter; fruit compote and ice cream; melted chocolate, banana and ice cream...

MAKES 8
PREP 30 MINUTES, PLUS
    OVERNIGHT CHILLING TIME
COOK 15 MINUTES

FOR THE GALETTES
about 100g butter, softened
1 egg, beaten
300ml whole milk
½ tsp salt
120g buckwheat flour
60g plain flour

FOR THE FILLING
8 thin slices of ham
120g gruyère cheese, finely
    grated
8 egg yolks

Melt 30g of the butter and allow to cool slightly. Using electric beaters – for reasons that will become clear – whisk the melted butter with the egg, 150ml of the milk, the salt and 300ml cool water in a large bowl. Gradually whisk in the flours to form a smooth batter. Keep whisking for a couple of minutes. You can do this by hand, first mixing the batter with a balloon whisk, then using the outstretched fingers of one hand to stir round, lift up and slap the batter down in a smooth motion. Continue for about four minutes. Either way, the batter should be smooth and elastic. Cover and chill overnight, or for up to 24 hours. Stir the remaining milk into the batter with 150ml water. The consistency should be somewhere close to single cream.

Heat a very large, non-stick frying pan or crêpe pan over a medium heat. Using kitchen paper, brush the surface with butter. Pour a small ladleful of batter into the pan, swirling it to cover the base thinly. Cook for about two minutes, until golden beneath and lacy at the edges. Use a spatula to flip over and cook for a minute more. Working swiftly, scrape with a smear of butter, a slice of ham and a nest of gruyère. Drop an egg yolk into the cheese and twist some pepper over. Cook until the yolk is setting at the edges. Flip in the edges to make a parcel and slide on to a plate. Repeat with the remaining ingredients to make eight folded galettes.

SUPPER
KOHLRABI SALAD

KOHLRABI, WHICH RESEMBLE FANTASTICAL GREEN OR PURPLE SPACESHIPS depending on the variety, are much underused. Their crisp flesh – akin to turnips but more like broccoli stalks in flavour – roasts, fries, stir-fries and braises very well but can also be stuffed or combined with celeriac in a mustardy rémoulade. Kohlrabi greens wilt down as well as any cabbage. I also think the bulb itself is an absolute winner in Thai and Vietnamese salads, shredded and generously dressed, with seared beef – thinly sliced – crushed peanuts, chillies and plenty of mint or Thai basil. Look for small kohlrabi, each no bigger than a cricket ball. At this time of year, the early, home-grown examples will be small with tender flesh, suited to slicing into rounds and eating uncooked. Delightful as it is, a Thai influence would feel incongruous in this menu, so I have gone with a simple and raw salad (with a resolutely European influence) to accompany the warm galettes.

Use a mandolin or, far more time consuming, a sharp knife to very finely slice the kohlrabi (a food processor slices a little too thickly for this job). Failing that, coarsely grate the flesh, wringing it out in a tea towel to get rid of any excess water.

Dress the kohlrabi, spring onions and chives generously with lime juice and olive oil, season and set aside for about five minutes. Tumble the watercress through just before serving

SERVES 8 AS A SIDE DISH
PREP 15 MINUTES

500g young, small kohlrabi, peeled
4 spring onions, very finely sliced
½ bunch of chives, finely snipped
good squeeze of lime juice
extra virgin olive oil
2 handfuls of watercress, large stems removed

A NOTE ON SLICING AND SHREDDING

The most unlikely vegetables can make excellent salad subjects if they are treated right. Consider a vegetable like a kohlrabi or celeriac; shaving whisper-thin slices or toothsome shreds gives them such interesting and versatile texture, rendering raw flesh – that would perhaps be too dense to tackle in large pieces – delicate and easy to eat. There are two pieces of equipment I find invaluable when making salads. Firstly, a small mandolin (such is my paranoia that I use the hand guard without fail) – nothing fancy, mine is just a cheap and light Japanese model from a local cookery shop – to make light work of slicing vegetables and fruit paper-thin. The other recommendation is a little shredder (officially known as a kiwi), resembling a swivel vegetable peeler with a serrated blade. You can pick one up for a song from any Vietnamese or Thai food shop to make light work of green papaya and the like for south east Asian salads.

LAID-BACK COUNTRY WEDDING FOR 20

With enough cake for many more...

SWEET PEPPER SAUSAGE ROLLS | HOME-SMOKED TROUT WITH CAPER MAYONNAISE | **SQUASH AND MANOURI SALAD** | *Summer barbecued roast of lamb* | BARBECUED ARTICHOKES WITH ALMONDS FOCACCIA BOARDS | SPLENDID STRAWBERRY AND VANILLA CAKE | *Drinks station: basil limeade; raspberry crush; elderflower vodka*

Catering for weddings instils fear into the hearts of even seasoned chefs. This is a menu for a charming and relaxed outdoor gathering, tiny by wedding standards (though everything except the cake can easily be doubled).

Slices of warm sausage roll, each enclosing a herbed pepper compote, will temper raging appetites before lunch. If a starter is called for, the smoked trout is eminently suitable, but the rest – the salad, lamb, artichokes and bread – can all be laid out, family-style, on a long table. Divide each between more than one serving dish and set them down the centre of the table, making sure to provide plenty of serving spoons.

The table only needs humble decoration. Summer flowers in multiple jam jars and small bottles look graceful and winsome. Fill two or three small tin baths, the kind found in antique shops and as quirky plant containers, with ice and water. Tuck them in the shade near to the table, evenly spaced along its length. They will serve as white wine, beer and champagne coolers. If you intend on returning any unopened bottles, keep them in the refrigerator rather than submerged in water, or the labels will peel off. An independent table serves as a drinks station for freshly made coolers and crushes.

In an attempt to free up the oven for sausage rolls and warming bread, the lamb is cooked via a slightly alternate method, first searing on a hot barbecue, then having a short blast in a hot oven, then being wrapped in foil and a thick blanket, where it sits, slowly cooking in the residual heat, for three to four hours. This is such a boon when cooking for large numbers; a few minutes extra resting won't hurt and the work has been done in advance.

The cake waits for dancers. It will sit patiently, in a very cool room, ready to be brought out and cut later in the day, once the music has started and a flood of extra guests have arrived.

SWEET PEPPER SAUSAGE ROLLS

THESE ARE RUSTIC SAUSAGE ROLLS, so don't expect them to look too pretty when they come out of the oven; their beauty is in their imperfection. Roasted sweet peppers and handfuls of herbs are baked into the rolls, providing a sort of integral relish. Only better. Serve them from wooden boards as people mill about, with a glass of champagne or a beer and plenty of napkins.

Preheat the oven to 220°C/fan 200°C/425°F/gas mark 7. Lay the pepper halves in a single layer across two baking sheets, skin-sides up. Drizzle with a little olive oil, to help the skins to blister. Roast for about 40 minutes, until truly blackened and soft. Tip the hot peppers into a bowl and cover it with a plate to keep the steam in. Set aside to cool until you can handle the peppers comfortably. Peel the skins off and throw them away. Slice the pepper flesh into rough strips and combine it with the chopped herbs, balsamic vinegar and a little salt and pepper. You can make this up to about four days in advance. Keep the peppers chilled. Reduce the oven temperature to 190°C/fan 170°C/375°F/gas mark 5.

Combine the egg yolk and milk in a cup to make an egg wash. Divide the pastry in half. On a lightly floured surface, roll the first block out to form a long, thin rectangle. Trim the edges to form a neat rectangle of about 15x40cm.

Divide the sausagemeat in half. Form the first half into a long sausage, the same length as the pastry rectangle. Dust with flour and lay on the pastry, about 4cm from one edge. Flatten the sausage slightly and top with half the roast pepper mixture. Roll the pastry around the sausage, sealing the edges with egg wash. Repeat with the remaining pastry and filling ingredients. Transfer both rolls to a large baking sheet. At this stage the rolls can be refrigerated overnight, just bring them up to room temperature before baking.

Brush both rolls generously with egg wash and diagonally slash the tops a few times, down the length of the roll. Bake for 35–40 minutes, until golden brown and well-risen. Slice the rolls into chunky pieces with a sharp, serrated knife and serve warm.

MAKES 2 LARGE ROLLS; EACH CUTS INTO 15–20 PIECES
PREP 50 MINUTES
COOK ABOUT 1¼ HOURS

7 mixed red, yellow or
  orange peppers, halved
olive oil
small handful each of basil,
  parsley and thyme, chopped
2 tbsp good-quality
  balsamic vinegar
1 egg yolk
2 tbsp milk
500g all-butter puff pastry
a little plain flour, to dust
1kg best-quality sausages,
  casings removed

HOME-SMOKED TROUT WITH CAPER MAYONNAISE

I STARTED WORK ON THIS CELEBRATORY RECIPE BY COOKING IT INDOORS, using a wok as a mini hot-smoker on the stove top. As the testing went on, however, I remembered why I rarely smoke meat and fish in this way any more: your house, curtains, clothes and hair will reek like a bonfire and only after a good few hours of airing the place – and at least one shower – will it begin to subside. Subsequently, the method I give below is for using a lidded barbecue as an outdoor hot-smoker. If you would like to explore the subject further, I give instructions on how to make your own hot-smoker on page 69.

The brief brining has several benefits. It will season, further preserve and, due to the sugar, tenderise the fish. After rinsing, the residual brine also hardens slightly when left to dry out, forming a protective surface to support the fish as it smokes and cooks.

All this smoking business does read as rather a bother but I promise you it is a fun process once you get the hang of it; the results are truly excellent and well worth the trouble. But if the point of the thing eludes you, simply use bought hot-smoked trout. You'll need about eight large trout fillets to serve this crowd with buttered squares of rye bread, watercress and dabs of caper mayonnaise. Ethereal fennel flowers bloom abundantly in these summer months. If you have a ready supply, add a few as (edible) finishing touches, their anise perfume complements trout beautifully.

ENOUGH FOR 20 AS A SUBSTANTIAL STARTER OR PART OF A BUFFET
PREP 30 MINUTES, PLUS BRINING
COOK 25–55 MINUTES

FOR THE CAPER MAYONNAISE

3 large egg yolks
150ml mild-flavoured olive oil, plus 3 tbsp more
300ml rapeseed or groundnut oil
2 tsp Dijon mustard
5 tbsp salted capers, rinsed and chopped
2 small bunches of parsley
lemon juice, to taste

Make the mayonnaise in advance. Using a food processor or a strong arm, briefly blend or whisk the egg yolks to break them down. Start adding the olive oil (reserving the extra 3 tbsp) drop by drop – no faster – with the blades (or whisk) whirring. As the oil is incorporated you may increase the drops to a very thin trickle, but don't go try to add it too fast or it could well split. Now start adding the rapeseed or groundnut oil, again gradually increasing the trickle as more is added, until the mayonnaise is thick and shiny and all the oil has been absorbed.

If the mixture splits, gradually whisk another egg yolk into the split mixture to bring it back and continue adding the oil as before, going more slowly this time.

Stir in the mustard and 3 tbsp of the chopped capers. Chop 2 tbsp of the parsley and stir this in too. Adjust the consistency and brighten the seasoning with a squeeze of lemon juice. Cover and chill for up to four days.

CONT...

FOR THE FISH

4 tbsp sea salt

4 tbsp brown sugar

1 tbsp cracked black pepper

4 large, fresh rainbow or brown
   trout, about 475-500g
   each, cleaned

TO SMOKE THE FISH

lidded barbecue, with coals and a
   metal grate

2 large handfuls of oak or apple
   woodchips

2 sheets of sturdy tin foil

TO SERVE

2 handfuls of watercress, washed
   and dried

20 large or 40 small slices of
   buttered rye bread

10 fennel flower heads (optional)

Now to the trout. They may be smoked up to five days in advance, then wrapped and chilled until needed.

Make the brine by mixing the salt, sugar and pepper with 500ml cool water. A lidded plastic container, big enough to hold the fish, is ideal for this. Submerge the gutted and scaled trout in the brine for one hour.

Rinse very briefly under cold running water – just to get rid of the excess salt – and dry the fish by patting them with kitchen paper. Meanwhile, light the barbecue coals and leave them to burn down until grey and glowing. No visible flame should remain. Dampen your sawdust or woodchips slightly then drop them in a border around the outer ring of coals. Scrunch up a double sheet of foil then cut or tear it to form a cup. Sit it in the centre of the coals, leaving the wood border exposed. Pour about 100ml water into this foil cup and sit the metal grate above.

Lay the trout on the grate and close the lid. Smoke for 40–50 minutes, but check after a mere 20 as both fish size and the heat from barbecue to barbecue will vary greatly. As soon as the flesh near the backbone flakes easily to the point of a knife, but remains slightly translucent and moist, remove the fish, grate and all. The skin will be burnished and golden around the belly. The trout will continue to cook a little more as they cool. Once cooled, they may be refrigerated or used straight away.

When lunchtime rolls around, lay your magnificent fish on large platters, ready to be skinned and flaked to order. Just before serving, heat the reserved 3 tbsp olive oil in a frying pan over a medium heat. Fry the reserved capers and parsley leaves until sizzling and crisp.

Spoon the hot caper and parsley mixture over and around the trout. Bowlfuls of caper mayonnaise, piles of watercress, buttered rye bread slices and those optional but decorative fennel flowers should all be offered alongside.

Hot home smoking, or 'real barbecue' in the US, is relatively easy to achieve at home; all you need is a lidded barbecue of sorts – whether bought or improvised – and a source of smoke.

By slowly barbecuing the food (be that fish, meat, poultry or vegetables) over smouldering, damp wood in a closed chamber, it will gently smoke as it cooks. Large, fatty cuts of meat are suited to home smoking, as it's a good treatment for a long cooking time and a lowish heat, very like firepit cooking (see pages 135–141). The fat will slowly render out, leaving extremely tender and succulent meat. In fact, the home smoker and the firepit have much in common, one simply happens to be above ground and the other below.

Choose a sweet wood as your smoke source. Cherry, apple and pear are all ideal, as is oak, though it creates a stronger smoke. Hickory chips or chunks are very strong, so use them sparingly or mix with other woods. Soak the wood in water for a few hours (a minimum of one hour is key); the more saturated the wood, the more smoke it will produce. You'll need about four logs for a standard, Weber-style lidded barbecue, or a couple of good double handfuls of wood chunks or chips (these should also be soaked and drained before use). I prefer logs as they smoulder far longer than chips or chunks, but any type will do.

Light the barbecue and wait for the coals to burn down to an ashen grey-white. Have the metal grate set as high up as possible, you don't want it too close to the coals or the food will scorch. Use tongs to scrape some of the coals aside, then throw the soaked wood into the centre. Rake some coals back on top of the wood. You should

have created a good supply of smoke. Fit the metal grate in place, set your chosen food on top and close the lid.

Cook fish until it gives to the touch. It will be firm, but should flake reluctantly. (For safe poultry and meat temperatures, see the chart on page 12 and use a meat thermometer to check.) Large joints will need a long cooking time; small cuts should be checked after 30 minutes and monitored from that time onwards. Cooking times will depend entirely on the heat of your barbecue. You will become an expert hot smoker with just a little practice, but it does take a couple of tries to get the knack.

It is possible to create a cold smoker by using far, far fewer coals – only a handful really – and smoking the food (this is particularly good for fish) for three to four hours. In this case, the temperature inside the barbecue should hover around 38°C (100°F). You may first want to brine meat or fish, or at least leave it uncovered in the fridge overnight, to form a tacky, hardened surface, known as a pellicule, which will protect the flesh below.

You can also use rosemary, thyme or bay branches to create smoke, just as you would with soaked wood logs, chunks or chips. Dampen the leaves, then throw them over ashen-grey coals to create a smoke that will imbue the food with a beautiful herbal taste.

SQUASH AND MANOURI SALAD

YOU MAY HAVE GLEANED, FROM A QUICK FLICK
THROUGH THESE PAGES, that I am fond of dense-fleshed squash,
especially when roasted. To defend my amour, it is dictated by head
as well as heart. A trayful of caramelised squash is one of the easiest,
and most versatile, solutions to feeding a crowd well, from soups,
stews and curries, to salads both warm and cool.

Greek delis are the most reliable source of manouri cheese, a fresh,
semi-soft white cheese, not dissimilar to a soft feta but with none
of its saltiness. With a lemon and dill dressing and a pinch of dried
chilli, it tastes fantastic. You could substitute feta that you have first
soaked in water for a few hours, or even better one of the great array
of manouri-like cheeses sold in good Middle Eastern food shops.
Verjuice I love. Deeply. It is pressed from unripe grapes and makes
a beautiful dressing, but don't panic if you can't find it; simply use
lemon juice and honey instead.

Preheat the oven to 200°C/fan 180°C/400°F/gas mark 6. Slice the
peeled squash in half, digging out the seeds with a spoon. Cut each
half into half-moons. Toss with the olive oil, season generously and
roast on two large, lined baking sheets for about 50 minutes, until
dark at the edges and tender. Turn carefully with a spatula halfway.
Leave to cool. This can be done two days beforehand and the squash
kept chilled and covered. Return to room temperature before using.

To make the dressing, whisk the extra virgin olive oil and verjuice
together (or replace the verjuice with honey and the juice of
1 lemon). Add the chilli flakes, fennel seeds and lemon zest. Stir in
half the chopped dill. Taste, season and taste again, then add more
verjuice or honey and lemon juice, if you want. Make this up to
three days in advance and keep it chilled, but only add the dill just
before using.

To serve, divide the remaining dill, the rocket, olives and roast
squash between two or three serving bowls. Whisk the dressing well
and spoon a little over each bowlful. Toss gently to coat the rocket
leaves lightly. Now add the manouri, gently distributing it among the
salad ingredients so as not to break the cheese up too much. Spoon
the remaining dressing evenly over each bowlful, sprinkle with a
little extra dried chilli, if you wish, and sea salt (remember that the
cheese contains no salt at all). Serve soon after.

**ENOUGH FOR 20 AS A SIDE
DISH, OR 10 AS A MAIN
COURSE**
PREP 20 MINUTES
COOK 45 MINUTES

FOR THE SALAD

2 large coquina or butternut
squash, peeled

5 tbsp olive oil

3 large handfuls of rocket

2 handfuls of large green olives
in oil, drained and stoned

600g manouri cheese, broken
into rough pieces

FOR THE DRESSING

175ml extra virgin olive oil

5 tbsp verjuice, or 2 tbsp liquid
honey, to taste

2 unwaxed lemons, finely grated
zest of both and juice to taste
(optional)

½ tsp chilli flakes, plus a pinch
to serve

2 tsp fennel seeds, lightly
crushed

large bunch of dill, chopped

SUMMER BARBECUED ROAST OF LAMB

THIS MAY SEEM A STRANGE RECIPE AT FIRST GLANCE, BUT I DEVELOPED IT from an old French technique I read about, to free up the oven and do away with any notions of tending a barbecue for hours. The lamb is first seared, then put in a hot oven, then left to finish cooking wrapped in a thick blanket. A large griddle pan or frying pan will suffice for searing the lamb if you don't have the wherewithal to barbecue it.

The herb paste is a gutsy cousin to salsa verde. Half is rubbed over the lamb before searing, half is let down with good olive oil and served alongside the cooked meat.

ENOUGH FOR 20 AS PART OF THIS MENU; EASILY HALVED TO SERVE 6–8 AS A MAIN COURSE
PREP 20 MINUTES
COOK 45 MINUTES, PLUS 3–4 HOURS 'RESTING'

FOR THE HERB PASTE
large bunch of chervil, roughly chopped
large bunch of parsley, roughly chopped
large bunch of basil, roughly chopped
10 fat garlic cloves, peeled
small can of anchovies in olive oil, drained
280g jar sundried tomatoes in oil, drained
4 red chillies, deseeded and roughly chopped
extra virgin olive oil, to loosen

2 large (around 2kg) lamb shoulders

No getting around it, unless you are a masterly and proficient chopper, this is a job for a food processor. Cram everything for the herb paste in with a hefty twist of pepper and only a pinch of salt (the anchovies are salty). Pour in about a wine glass of olive oil – enough to get the blades moving, in other words – then press the pulse button, stopping to scrape everything down the sides a couple of times. You're aiming for a rusty red 'salsa verde' with a thick but nubbly texture. Scoop half the mixture into a bowl and stir in more olive oil to loosen. This will be your sauce, to serve with the lamb, so cling film the top and chill it for up to five days, until needed. The rest will serve as a herb paste, to rub over the lamb shoulders. Of course, this can also be kept for a few days before using.

Rub the thick portion of the herb paste over the lamb shoulders, covering the entire surface. Preheat the oven to 220°C/fan 200°C/425°F/gas mark 7. Light the barbecue and wait until the coals are white hot and glowing in places. Quickly sear each lamb shoulder on the metal grate, until beginning to char on the outside, for no more than 10 minutes. You want to imbue the lamb with smoke, not cook it. Transfer both shoulders to a large roasting tin.

Roast in the preheated oven for 30 minutes. The lamb will be well-coloured but shouldn't be burnt. Immediately cover the tin in four layers of thick tin foil, sealing the edges tightly and trapping the heat in. Now wrap in a thick blanket or a few old towels. Set aside for three hours for rare; four hours for medium-rare. The shoulders will hold for an hour or so longer, if needed. Unwrap the lamb and slice each shoulder thickly on a board. Serve with the herb sauce.

BARBECUED ARTICHOKES WITH ALMONDS

THOSE YOUNG, PURPLE ARTICHOKES ARE SUCH A TREAT but preparing them is, quite frankly, a sod. Large globe artichokes are far more amenable, proving greater square footage for the effort of trimming them and removing the choke. I stumbled upon this way of preparing them on the barbecue. The slightly blackened but tender artichokes work so well with a simple dressing and a handful of toasted almonds.

Start by whisking the garlic, balsamic vinegar, mustard and olive oil together. This can be done a few days in advance and kept chilled.

Cut the top third from each artichoke, just enough so you can dig down with a teaspoon and pull out the hairy choke from the centre. With a small paring knife, pare away the tough outside of the stalk and any tough leaves at the bottom. Stick a bay leaf into the centre.

Make sure the barbecue coals are white hot, with no trace of flame. Wrap each artichoke tightly in foil and barbecue over indirect heat for 20–25 minutes. Once unwrapped, the artichokes should be tender and slightly charred at the edges.

Serve warm or cool, with a generous amount of dressing spooned over – concentrating on the centres – and the almonds and parsley scattered on top. The tops of the leaves will not be edible (the bases are) and need to be pulled away from the artichoke to eat, so provide a few fingerbowls with lemon slices.

ENOUGH FOR UP TO 10 WITH THE SALADS, IN PLACE OF THE LAMB
PREP 30 MINUTES
COOK 20–25 MINUTES

FOR THE DRESSING
1 garlic clove, crushed
4 tbsp good balsamic vinegar
1 tsp wholegrain mustard
175ml extra virgin olive oil

FOR THE ARTICHOKES
10 globe artichokes
10 bay leaves
100g flaked almonds, toasted
handful of parsley, chopped

FOCACCIA BOARDS

When catering for large numbers, one occasionally has to compromise. Baking your own bread is obviously to be applauded. And yet... What with smoking fish and cooking on a barbecue and all the other bits and pieces, something has to give.

Get to know a local deli or baker stocking or producing good bread. Focaccia is lovely with this menu but any rustic or crusty bread would do well. Get somebody to bring them for you on the morning of your event. I reckon to serve one large focaccia between four people within a menu such as this. Slice them no more than 30 minutes before they will be needed, covering with tea towels. Set up at least one 'bread area' in the shade, with a wooden chopping board to pile the loaves on. Spoon butter into small dishes and stand butter knives in jam jars. You'll need extra virgin olive oil for dipping, too. That way, you don't need to get involved in the business of serving it. A hand-painted sign is a nice touch; it need only say 'bread' and can be as wonky as you like.

Having worked as a food stylist for many years, I have picked up a fair few ideas along the way. Here are some practical tips and styling touches intended only to inspire; hopefully they tread a line that is charming and attainable, without being prissy. Remember that good food and a happy party are the most important things, so don't get even remotely het up about decoration schemes.

SEATING

It is important that everybody sits comfortably. That way, they will be relaxed and more inclined to enjoy the food. Simple cotton or linen seat pads can be made by covering foam pads or slim cushions with fabric. Even a very basic muslin or curtain lining will look fabulous for very little outlay. Sew ties at two corners, to tie the seat pad to the chair; they will make any chair cooler and more comfortable.

Use whatever chairs you can find: plastic, wicker, padded, wooden, always with the mindset that mismatching is a charming bonus. Even becushioned tree stumps look weirdly wonderful. If you are holding a wedding or similar celebration, swathes of slightly stiff fabric, tied around the chair backs in a bow, look very grand.

Sitting comfortably certainly doesn't have to involve chairs. Mezze night's Moroccan-ish menu (see page 175), for example, lends itself superbly to lounging on big cushions on a rug. The food could be set out on a low table in the middle, or simply laid out on the rug with everybody sitting around, picnic-style.

In desperate times, if the table is too small and you can't source enough chairs, you could sling a couple of planks (nothing splintery!) across the seats of at least three chairs so people can sit in between. You'll need a sturdy chair at each end and at least one to take the strain in the centre. Leave no more than a generously seated bottom's length between each chair, for safety. Make it comfier with cushions and use magazines to even up any discrepancies in chair height, so everything is stable.

Try not to let things get so cramped that lifting a fork or an elbow is a battle; if space is that short it would be far better to extend the tables slightly.

TABLES

Whether round or rectangular, if at all possible, it's best to keep the seating to one table, so go for 'bolt-on' tables where you can. Obviously, with numbers above a dozen, it's going to be tricky in most houses. In that case, keep the tables as close as you can without cramping anybody.

Trestle tables, constructed with a pair of saw-horses and a sturdy sheet of plywood, can be set up. Check the stability multiple times. If the table is on a lawn or soft ground, be prepared to put sheets of plywood down to form a temporary base. It will stop table legs, chairs and high heels sinking into the grass.

Tablecloths in the same fabric or similar colours do a great job of bringing everything together and hiding any joins or formica that lie beneath.

BLOSSOM & BLOOM

Flowers on the table are the simplest, but most effective, decoration I know. Nothing should obscure anybody's view, nor take up too much space. Put just a few seasonal flowers into old jam jars, empty tea caddies, tin cans or tin spice pots and set them on the table. In autumn, use catkins or hardy herbs.

Separate children's tables are a fabulous idea. I remember delighting in the separate table my cousins and I shared at family gatherings. Leave the oldest child in charge and keep an eye on proceedings...

DRINKS STATIONS

I like to keep drinks separate from the food, if at all possible, to keep queues and people-traffic to a minimum.

On a completely separate table, set up extra glasses or jam jars for cocktails and cordials. Have them lined up, complete with jaunty straws and ice in a chilled bowl. The cocktail ingredients – or cordials and soda – can be poured to taste. The table will look so pretty and it will simplify matters greatly.

LANTERNS & CANDLES

Fairy lights cover a multitude of sins after dark; string them up in trees, or over walls and canopies.

Lanterns, hung safely from branches or on sticks, make for a romantic evening setting. For an inexpensive alternative, try punching holes in empty tin cans, using thick gloves, a screwdriver and a hammer, to make pretty tealight holders. Add string loops to the top to hang them by. Light the way to or from supper with bought paper lanterns, homemade tin can lanterns (as above) or glass lanterns, made by covering the bases of jam jars with sand and standing slim

candles up in them. Citronella candles and torches will keep insects at bay on summer evenings.

Those globular white or coloured paper lanterns so beloved by students can be bought in varying sizes, ready to be strung and hung from trees. They will look beautiful in the daytime as well as at night and make the prettiest garlands. As, would you believe, do coffee filters. The unbleached or white filters can be bunched together and sewn through the centre, or tied, to form a ruffled 'flower'. String these blossoms up on a length of twine or ribbon, to form a garland for very little cost. Coffee filters are also useful as liners for bowls of fruit, truffles, cakes or brownies.

SEATING PLANS

I only bother with these when more than six guests are involved, or when trying to matchmake without being crashingly obvious. It does create a sense of formality, which isn't always a good thing, but you can have some fun in the planning and hopefully make sure conversation hums along energetically, if not nicely, on the day or night.

OTHER IDEAS

Slim wooden stakes, plunged into the ground, look ethereally lovely with fine strips of lightweight fabric tied to the tips. They will dance in the breeze.

Garden twine is invaluable for bunching, tying, stringing up lights, lanterns and tealight jars and for grouping chopsticks, cutlery or napkins. Raffia or strips of muslin also do the job with the latter three.

Soften candles and jars by tying a scrap of cloth – something light and loose such as muslin is ideal – around the centre and knotting it loosely.

If you're sitting outside and it's a chilly evening, offer blankets for those who feel the cold to drape over their laps.

Finishing Touches

Put your cynical tendencies aside and go with this (unless we're talking about getting the boys round to watch the rugby and scarf down a curry), because a few personal touches, which can be as simple as you like, really do create a sense of occasion.

The idea may seem a little gussied-up, but place settings are a sweet way to seat guests where you want them and pay homage to whatever season you find yourselves in. I am a great fan of using single fruits or vegetables, or simple objects. Tie an old-fashioned postal label – the pale grey sort with a punched hole and string ties – around the stalk or girth of said object, having first written names on them.

No time or wish to lay the table formally? Stick tied bundles of cutlery into small buckets or kilner jars and space them out on the table when you get a second, ready for guests to help themselves. Or, in each water tumbler, stick a napkin, a tied knife, fork and spoon and a name tag. Perhaps a fresh blossom, too.

If you're hosting a large gathering and don't want to keep on shouting what everything is, make labels and/or write a menu. It needn't be a work of art, just your best writing on some nice card or paper is fine. Go to town if you like though; an old typewriter makes delightful labels and menus. That way, everyone knows what's what and it is a fun touch.

SOME SUGGESTIONS:

SPRING AND SUMMER
Bunch of cherries
Sprig of lilac
*Pre-dinner cocktail in a jam jar,
    with a striped straw*
Heirloom tomato
Paper fan
Globe artichoke
Bunch of fresh rosemary or thyme
A single shell
An old-fashioned English rose

AUTUMN AND WINTER
Mini pumpkin
Small bunch of grapes
A perfect fig
*A tiny, sealed jar of marmalade
    or citrus curd*
*Clementine or Sicilian lemon,
    with leaves*
Cinnamon stick
Pine cone
Small pomegranate

SPLENDID STRAWBERRY AND VANILLA CAKE

**SERVES 50–90 (SEE RECIPE
    INTRODUCTION)**
PREP 3½ HOURS
COOK ABOUT 3½ HOURS

YOU WILL NEED:

3 deep, springform cake tins of
    26cm, 23cm and 20cm

FOR THE BASE CAKE

475g caster sugar
475g unsalted butter, very soft
8 eggs, at room temperature
550g self-raising flour
1 ½ tsp baking powder
½ tsp salt
75g ground almonds
100ml buttermilk
2½ tsp vanilla extract

FOR THE MIDDLE CAKE

350g caster sugar
350g unsalted butter, very soft
6 eggs, at room temperature
400g self-raising flour
½ tsp baking powder
generous pinch of salt
50g ground almonds
75ml buttermilk
1 ½ tsp vanilla extract

FOR THE TOP CAKE

175g caster sugar
175g unsalted butter, very soft
3 eggs, at room temperature
200g self-raising flour
¼ tsp baking powder
pinch of salt
25g ground almonds
40ml buttermilk
¾ tsp vanilla extract

NOW THIS IS A PROJECT.

We fruit cake haters have to stick to our guns. I would infinitely prefer to eat this fresh, rather informal cake at a wedding or summer celebration than any marzipan. Its vanilla sponge has to be sturdy enough to hold up to being split and stacked but, in spite of this, the cake remains light to eat. The recipe is easily divided so, if you only want to make one tier, just pick your size.

Black flecks of vanilla seed speckle the ivory icing. To get the same effect without vanilla pods, substitute 3 tsp of vanilla bean paste (Taylor and Colledge make an easy-to-find one).

Slicing wedding cakes is a particular art. Work from the outside in, dividing the cake by eye into a central circle and a surrounding ring. The surrounding ring is cut into approximately 3x5cm slices; the central circle is divided into small wedges. Working on this principal makes a rather scary total of 90 slices. Realistically however, accounting for less-than expert cutting, it will give a slightly more reasonable 80 servings. If you are more generous with your portions, reckon on the cake serving 50–60. Leftovers freeze beautifully.

Preheat the oven to 170°C/fan 150°C fan/350°F/gas mark 3½. Line the bases and sides of the three tins with non-stick baking parchment, sticking it in place with tiny dabs of butter.

The method is the same for each cake: with the paddle attachment fitted on a food mixer, beat the sugar and butter until pale and light. You can also do this with a wooden spoon and an energetic arm. Add the eggs, one-by-one, as you continue to beat. If the mixture looks curdled, add a spoonful of the flour and continue to beat. Sift the flour and baking powder over and throw in the salt. With the speed on very low, mix, stopping to scrape down the sides, until the dry ingredients are just incorporated. Add the almonds, buttermilk and vanilla, before briefly mixing to form a firm batter. Scrape into the tin, flattening out the batter with a spatula, then make a shallow dip in the centre. This accounts for the cake rising in the middle.

Bake in the centre of the oven, leaving well alone for the first 45 minutes at least, lest the cake collapses when you open the door. Bake the largest cake for about 1½ hours, the middle cake for about 1 hour 10 minutes and the small cake for about 55 minutes. They should be golden and well risen. When a skewer is inserted, it should come out clean. Let the cakes rest in their tins for a few minutes, then turn out on to wire racks and leave to cool completely.

CONT...

FOR THE ICING

500g unsalted butter, very soft
1kg cream cheese, such as
    Philadelphia, at room
    temperature
2 vanilla pods, split and seeds
    scraped out, or 3 tsp vanilla
    paste or extract
900g icing sugar, sifted, or
    to taste

**FOR THE FILLING AND
    TOPPING**

600g good-quality strawberry
    jam
800g strawberries, hulled
    and sliced

It is highly likely you won't want to fill the cakes straight away. They will keep, well wrapped, for a couple of days. Any more than that and I would advise you to freeze them. Beg or borrow freezer space from a cake-hating neighbour if you don't have enough yourself. Wrap in several layers of cling film and freeze for up to three months. Defrost slowly overnight when needed.

The cream cheese icing can be made up to five days ahead and kept in a sealed container (or several containers, considering the amount) in the refrigerator. The most important point is that the butter must be very soft and the cream cheese must be at room temperature. If one or both are too cold, they will not whip to a smooth icing and you may get tiny pebbles of hard butter suspended throughout.

With the paddle attachment in place, beat the butter and cream cheese together in an electric mixer. Keep beating for about four minutes, stopping to scrape down the sides of a bowl with a spatula. Add the vanilla seeds, paste or extract with the mixer running.

Turn the speed down very low and slowly add the icing sugar. If you add it too quick, a sugar cloud will surround you. Keep adding until all the sugar is incorporated, then taste for sweetness. If you prefer a more sugary icing, add 100–300g more, remembering that the cake and jam filling are already sweet. The more sugar you add, the thicker the icing will become. Increase the speed for the last few seconds, to give the icing a last whip. Use straightaway or cover and chill for later use. (Chilled icing is easier to work with.)

Carefully split the cakes in half with a serrated knife, taking off any risen 'domes' at the same time, if necessary. Have the jam and strawberries to hand. The cakes will sit upside down to make them easier to ice and neater to present, meaning the top half of each will now become the base and vice versa.

Spread the lower half of the largest cake with a 2cm or so layer of cream cheese icing, leaving a small border at the edge to allow for the icing squidging out when the top half is applied. Cover with a tightly wedged layer of sliced strawberries, again, being mindful that they won't bulge out of the sides later. Spread the top half with jam, again leaving a small border at the edge. Place this on top of the base cake and press gently to seal. Run a layer of icing around the outside of the middle join, to seal in the jam and strawberries and prevent any pink bleeding out.

Repeat with the remaining two cakes.

A tiered design such as this needs support to prevent the cake from collapsing, which is where the dowelling comes in. Measure one rod against the largest cake and mark the height of the cake. Cut into three or four equal lengths. Do the same with the next dowelling rod and the middle cake. Stick three or four vertical rods into each of the larger cakes. They should be evenly spaced and hidden within the cake. If they stick up at all, trim them down.

Using a palette knife, spread a very thin layer of icing over the sides of all three cakes, making it slightly thicker when you spread it over the tops. It doesn't have to be neat. This is called the crumb layer and traps any crumbs that could disrupt the finish of the iced cake. If the entire cake is to be served from a large wooden board, you will need no cake board beneath. If you intend to present it on a cake stand, the safe move is to first sit the base tier on the cake board. I must confess I don't always do this and haven't come a cropper yet...

Once the largest cake is sitting on its chosen base, cut or tear four wide strips of baking paper. Tuck the long sides of all these strips just underneath the cake, to form a wide border all the way around the base, to protect the surface below as you spread the icing on.

Sit the middle cake on top, off-centre, so that one vertical edge lines up with a vertical edge of the large cake. Do the same with the top tier, lining the 'back' of the entire cake up carefully, it should be completely vertical with no similarities to a certain tower from Pisa. The finished arrangement will be like three steps. Stick the remaining wooden dowel vertically through the three cakes, from top to bottom. Trim any excess so that it is completely hidden.

Dollop icing on to the top of the top cake. Working in confident, sweeping motions, work the icing over and across the top to the edges. Now work the overspill around the sides, keeping the knife almost vertical to create a clean finish. Keep adding more icing as needed and sweeping it across and down until the entire three cakes are covered thickly and evenly. You will need to spend quite a bit of time walking around the cake and viewing it from every angle to check no sponge is showing. Keep the cake cool: sun and heat are the enemies of cream cheese icing, though curious pets come a close second. The iced cake will sit in the cool for a few hours without harm. Even overnight is not out of the question, in a cold larder.

Just before serving, decorate the cake sparingly with fresh, unsprayed flowers, wild strawberries and wild strawberry leaves. Less is more.

YOU WILL NEED:

3 x 30cm wooden or plastic dowelling rods, ready to cut to size

thin 30cm diameter cake board (optional)

baking parchment, to assist with icing the cake

fresh, unsprayed roses, sweet pea flowers, wild strawberries and strawberry leaves, to decorate

Serve with aplomb. You'll need trusted helpers to share the carrying. Walk slowly! And well done. This is a cake to be incredibly proud of.

DRINKS STATION: BASIL LIMEADE, RASPBERRY CRUSH AND ELDERFLOWER VODKA

ADORN A SEPARATE TABLE WITH ICE BOWLS, soda, extra glasses, stirrers and muddlers. Set labelled jugs of these drinks out and direct your guests to the table with a drinks sign and an arrow. It's a good idea to have somebody man the station, ready to top up the levels, and to keep the elderflower vodka away from the kids...

ENOUGH FOR 20 TALL (DILUTED) GLASSES, EASILY HALVED
PREP 20 MINUTES, PLUS COOLING

750g granulated sugar
2 large handfuls of Greek basil or chopped standard basil leaves
juice of 24 limes
still or sparking water, to top up
4 limes, sliced, to serve
ice cubes, to serve

BASIL LIMEADE

I have used Greek basil to make this fresh limeade with excellent results, though chopped basil of the normal kind is perfectly fine. This recipe also works well with mint.

Put the sugar in a large saucepan with 1 litre of water and one large handful of basil. Bring to the boil slowly, stirring to dissolve the sugar. Once no grains of sugar remain, turn off the heat. Set aside to cool, then strain through a fine sieve.
Combine the sugar syrup with the lime juice and dilute with still or sparkling water to taste. Serve in jugs with the lime slices, remaining basil leaves and ice if you like.

ENOUGH FOR 20
PREP 15 MINUTES

600g ripe raspberries
juice of 8 lemons
150g caster sugar
chilled lemonade or sparkling water, to top up
Chambord (optional)

RASPBERRY CRUSH

This is a great one for kids (without the Chambord). If the rustic crushed raspberries bother you, strain them out before diluting.

In a large mixing bowl, crush the raspberries, lemon juice and sugar with a potato masher. Leave to macerate for 10 minutes, then divide between two jugs and top up with lemonade or sparkling water (depending on how sweet you like your drinks). Adults could add a little Chambord, that delightfully tacky raspberry liqueur.

ENOUGH FOR 20
PREP 10 MINUTES

500ml elderflower cordial
1 litre good-quality vodka
juice of 15 limes
ice cubes, to serve

ELDERFLOWER VODKA

A cheeky little cocktail number that you can serve straight, over ice, or top up with soda water in tall, ice-filled glasses.

Combine the cordial, vodka and lime juice. Chill until needed. Serve over ice, as it is, or diluted with sparkling water.

GLAMPING

A HEARTY VEGETABLE SOUP | **SMOKY PEA AND HAM SOUP** | *Pressed steak or antipasti sandwiches* | **RED ONION RELISH WITH PORT** | DEEP AND CHEWY FLAPJACKS | **LEMON AND CARDAMOM CHICKEN THIGHS** | GEORGINA'S TOASTED COUSCOUS WITH GREEN LEAVES

There is a world of difference between glamping – glamorous camping to you and I – and proper, hardy camping. In turn, there is a great deal of difference between glamping in the great outdoors and boutique camping, at music festivals. I wouldn't be so foolish as to suggest you trek over hill and dale with a two-man tent on your back and whip up a vegetable soup for your supper. More likely a can of tepid baked beans in that situation. But at least the flapjacks will provide trekking fuel, so all is not lost.

What I'm getting at is camping with a few creature comforts; with comfy beds and cool boxes, or mini refrigerators plugged into an electric hook up; with camper vans or in a spacious bell tent. Camping for softies and not the real, rugged deal, in other words.

These recipes are mostly intended to be made before you leave, so you have some good food to get you started. A couple, namely the pressed sandwiches and sticky chicken with couscous and greens, depend on some sort of cooler to keep them chilled for a few hours. Unless transported in a Thermos, the soups will need to be reheated over a camping stove.

As for music festivals, I know how this one goes. Before you know it, you'll be drinking lemonade for breakfast and eating chocolate for lunch and, by supper time, you'll either be in front of a stage, or you'll be enticed over to the plethora of gourmet burger and noodle stalls that most large festivals boast. The trouble being that the festival tickets, travel and paraphernalia cost at least a week's wages, so you might not have fistfuls of money to burn. At least you can take a good soup along, or a sandwich, or a batch of flapjacks. Something homemade and wholesome to keep you ticking along for a day at least. Just wait until day three, when cold beans from a can will seem practically gourmet...

❧FOOD❧

1 A good amount of **drinking water**.
2 Flapjacks (*see page 92*) or similarly dense cereal bars, cakes and biscuits.
3 A fabulous **sandwich**, kept cool with a freezer block, for the first day only. One that won't mind getting squashed (*see page 91*).

4 Apples, dried fruit and nuts as a slightly healthier source of energy. Don't take bananas; they will get squashed.
5 Baked beans.
6 Bread. Something that will keep for a day or two, such as sourdough.

7 Cooking oil in a small bottle.
8 Marshmallows.
9 Salt, pepper, ketchup.

COOKING & Food Kit

1 A light **cool bag** with frozen freezer blocks for milk, juice, cheese, bacon and so on.
2 Matches or a lighter.
3 a) **Fire lighters** to encourage damp wood to burn b) Or a **camping stove** with gas.

4 Billy cans or light cooking pans.
5 An **oven glove** or thick cloth.
6 Washing-up liquid and a scourer.
7 Long tongs and a **wooden spoon**.

8 Camping plates/bowls, basic cutlery, mugs or cups.
9 A **pocket knife**. Opinels are beautiful.
10 A **vegetable peeler**.

...AND DON'T LEAVE HOME WITHOUT

1 Sunscreen.
2 A torch.
3 Bin liners for rubbish.
4 Anti-bac hand wipes.

A HEARTY VEGETABLE SOUP

INSTEAD OF BARLEY, YOU COULD USE QUINOA, it won't need any pre-cooking so can be added to the olive oil with the vegetables. A grain or grass of some sort adds extra bolster and nourishment that will be especially welcome when an energy boost is needed. This soup needs no accompaniment.

Extras freeze perfectly for a few months. Although the vegetables need to be finely diced to make them easy to eat, I don't bother to skin the tomatoes and I see no need to remove their seeds. This is a hearty soup, not a dinner party soup (I don't think I'd want one of those anyway). If you want to use a can of plum tomatoes instead of fresh, smush them down a little and add halfway through the simmering time to cook out any 'tinny' taste.

The soup will keep, chilled, for a good five days. Reheat until piping hot, but you can allow it to cool and eat at room temperature if it's a very hot day. This is actually a nicer idea than it may sound!

Cover the barley with plenty of water in a saucepan, add a pinch of salt and bring to the boil. Cover and simmer gently for 15 minutes, then drain and set aside.

Heat the olive oil in a large saucepan and add all the vegetables except the spinach, broad beans and tomatoes. Season with a little salt to draw the water out and gently cook, stirring often, for 10 minutes, until softened but not coloured.

Add the stock and par-cooked barley and bring to the boil. Reduce the heat to the point where the soup is simmering nicely. Leave to simmer for 30 minutes, then add the spinach, broad beans and tomatoes and continue to simmer for a further five to 10 minutes. Remove from the heat and stir in the basil. Taste and adjust the seasoning as needed, then serve or ladle into large flasks, or cool and chill, ready to re-heat later.

I very much doubt this would be the case at a festival, but if you make this at home and have any good extra virgin olive oil to hand, or even better, fresh pesto, add a little to each serving before eating.

SERVES 8
PREP 20 MINUTES
COOK ABOUT 1 HOUR

200g pearl barley or spelt

3 tbsp olive oil

1 large fennel bulb, trimmed and finely chopped

12 smallish, young carrots, scrubbed and finely diced

12 new potatoes, scrubbed and finely diced

6 courgettes, trimmed and finely diced

bunch of spring onions, trimmed and finely sliced

1 litre good vegetable stock

1kg spinach leaves, washed and drained

200g fresh or frozen young broad beans (podded weight)

6 plum tomatoes, diced

handful of basil leaves, shredded (optional)

SMOKY PEA AND HAM SOUP

SERVES 8 GENEROUSLY,
   MORE IF YOU SERVE
   IN MUGS
PREP 15 MINUTES, PLUS 1 TO 4
   HOURS SOAKING
COOK 1¼ HOURS

1 smoked ham hock
1 large onion, roughly chopped
1 large carrot, roughly chopped
2 celery sticks, roughly chopped
bouquet garni of 2 bay leaves,
   2 sprigs of thyme and 2 sprigs
   of rosemary
300g green or yellow split peas
400g fresh or frozen green peas,
   shelled weight

EVEN SUMMER NIGHTS CAN GET CHILLY – especially
when the inevitable drizzle gets the better of the sun – but a mug of
soup, made a day or two in advance and heated up when needed,
will ward off the damp. This is a London Particular for the summer
months, made brighter and lighter with a good helping of fresh or
frozen peas.
A ham hock can be ridiculously salty, so be sure to soak it in plenty
of cold water before cooking. At least one to four hours of soaking,
with a couple of water changes, will prevent any excess salt from
spoiling your soup.

Soak the ham hock as mentioned in the recipe introduction. When
ready to make the soup, put everything apart from the fresh or
frozen green peas in a large, lidded saucepan with 1.6 litres of water
and bring to the boil. Reduce the heat to low and leave to putter-
putter gently, lid on, for an hour and a half. Add the fresh or frozen
peas and cook for a further five minutes. Turn the heat off and
remove the bouquet garni, then carefully fish out the ham hock,
dropping it into a bowl.

Allow the hock to cool a little before shredding or chopping the
meat quite finely, removing and discarding the skin, fat and bone as
you go. Set aside.

Purée the soup in the pan with a stick blender, or pour into an
upright blender in two batches. I don't purée this thoroughly, so the
soup retains some texture, but blitz until smooth if you prefer.

Return the soup to the heat, along with all but 3 tbsp of the
shredded ham, if you will be garnishing the soup, otherwise just add
it all now. Taste and add more salt if needed, it will certainly need a
little black pepper. Let down with water if the soup seems too thick
to you, the consistency is supposed to be hearty though, not thin.

Serve hot, scattered with the reserved ham if the circumstances
warrant garnish and fripperies. The soup will keep chilled for up to
five days; reheat until piping hot before eating.

PRESSED STEAK OR ANTIPASTI SANDWICHES

INSTEAD OF FILLING INDIVIDUAL LOAVES or sandwiches, you can hollow out one large loaf, fill it with the ingredients and press for a few hours before slicing and eating.

If you are using small loaves of bread, cut them in half and pull out most of the doughy crumb with your fingers, leaving a sturdy shell. The middles make excellent breadcrumbs, so freeze for another day.

Place a griddle or frying pan over a high heat until smoking hot. Rub the steaks with a little olive oil and the rosemary. Season generously. Sear the steaks in the hot pan, literally for just a minute each side, until browned but still medium rare. Remove to a plate and leave to cool. Slice each steak into four and reserve the juices.

Drizzle the insides of the loaves, or one side of each bread slice, with olive oil. Layer four loaf bases or bread slices (oiled side up), a spoonful of steak juices (not too much or it will get soggy), 1 tbsp red onion relish, 6 pieces of steak and some rocket. Layer the other four with the antipasti vegetables, mozzarella and basil leaves.

Replace all the loaf tops or top with a second slice of bread (oiled side down) and wrap each firmly in cling film. Place a weight (such as a can of beans) on top of each and leave to press in the refrigerator for two to five hours before unwrapping and eating.

MAKES 8 ROLLS OR SANDWICHES
PREP 20 MINUTES, PLUS 2 TO 5 HOURS PRESSING
COOK 2 MINUTES

8 small, rustic loaves of bread, or 16 thin slices of rustic bread
extra virgin olive oil

FOR THE STEAK
6 minute steaks
1 tsp finely chopped rosemary
4 tbsp Red Onion Relish with Port (see below)
handful of wild rocket leaves

FOR THE ANTIPASTI
300g antipasti (chargrilled peppers, artichokes, aubergines, or tomatoes in oil, drained weight)
2 balls buffalo mozzarella, drained thoroughly and sliced
handful of basil leaves

RED ONION RELISH WITH PORT

A NATTY LITTLE NUMBER to have up your sleeve. You can also add this to stews, gravies and meaty sauces for a touch of sweetness.

Add the onions to a very large saucepan with the oil and salt. Cook over a low heat for a couple of minutes, then cover tightly and cook for 40 minutes, stirring occasionally. Remove the lid and add the port, increasing the heat slightly. Let the liquid bubble away, stirring to stop it catching, then tip in the sugar and stir until the onions begin to turn golden. This will take longer than you think! Finish with the vinegar and thyme, again, cooking until the liquid has gone.

Pot in sterilised jars – sealing them tightly – and keep in the refrigerator. Aim to use within a month or so.

MAKES 2 LARGE JAM JARS
PREP 20 MINUTES
COOK ABOUT 1 HOUR 40 MINUTES

2kg red onions, halved and finely sliced
2 tbsp olive oil
large pinch of salt
250ml port
90g caster sugar
4 tbsp balsamic vinegar
2 tbsp thyme leaves

DEEP AND CHEWY FLAPJACKS

BEST NOT TO KID YOURSELF ABOUT THE FACTS HERE: this ain't no diet food. Flapjacks are no more than oats suspended in butter toffee... last time I looked, that combination wasn't high on the list of recommended health foods. But they are incredibly good. These enormous ones are perfect for sharing and will fuel a great deal of rainy festival-traipsing. Reasons enough to make them, without the pseudo cereal bar label, I hope.

Do replace some of the oats with seeds, nuts or dried fruit if you would like to add more interest to this delightfully plain version.

MAKES 12 RIDICULOUSLY LARGE FLAPJACKS, OR 16 SLIGHTLY MORE REASONABLE ONES
PREP 10 MINUTES
COOK 1 HOUR 10 MINUTES

650g butter
350g brown sugar
360g golden syrup
400g jumbo rolled oats
300g porridge oats (I use half spelt)
pinch of salt

Preheat the oven to 150°C/fan 130°C/300°F/gas mark 2. Use a convection rather than a fan oven, if possible.

In your largest pan, melt the butter, sugar and syrup together over a low heat, stirring until no grains of sugar remain. Keep cooking and stirring until the toffee is bubbling and smooth. Stir in all the oats and continue to stir over the heat for five minutes. You want them to soften in the toffee. Mix in the salt and turn off the heat.

Press firmly into a 30x20cm tin, lined with non-stick baking parchment that reaches up the sides. Bake for 1 hour 10 minutes, or until deeply golden at the edges but still a tiny bit wobbly right in the centre.

Dip a wooden spoon in cold water (to stop it sticking) and use the back to press the flapjack down again firmly. Set aside to cool in the tin; it's very important that you don't disturb, score or cut the flapjacks now or they won't hold together. Leave them to get completely cool. That means overnight for best results, or a minimum of four hours if you're really in a pickle.

Tip the whole flapjack out on to a board, remove the paper and cut into as many pieces as you desire. They'll last in an airtight tin, in a cool place, for up to a week.

LEMON AND CARDAMOM CHICKEN THIGHS

SERVES 4 HUNGRY PEOPLE
PREP 15 MINUTES, PLUS
   MARINATING
COOK 45 MINUTES

4 tbsp extra virgin olive oil

4 tbsp runny honey

2 garlic cloves, crushed

finely grated zest of 2 unwaxed
   lemons and juice of 1

6 green cardamom pods, crushed
   so they split

1 tsp coarsely ground
   black pepper

8 large chicken thighs (or legs),
   with bone and skin

1 tbsp sesame seeds

MAKE YOUR PEACE WITH THE PICNICKER'S (COLD) CHICKEN, for the skin will have lost much of its crunch. I still think it delicious, in the way that brined and ready-cooked chicken is. If you are making these to eat hot, the skin will be crisp and generally most appealing.

Incidentally, it's quite possible to make this on a camping stove, keeping the heat low to cook the chicken right through. But, in the absence of camping paraphernalia, I'd recommend cooking the thighs in advance. Chill them down thoroughly and transport chicken, couscous and greens (see right) in airtight containers, tucked into a padded cool bag and buffered by a couple of small ice blocks. It should keep you away from those expensive burger vans for a few more hours at least.

Marinate the chicken. In a non-metallic, ovenproof dish, combine all the ingredients except the sesame seeds with a large pinch of salt. Cover and chill for at least eight hours, or up to two days.

Preheat the oven to 220°C/fan 200°C/425°F/gas mark 7. Turn the chicken pieces skin-side up, baste well and slide into the oven. Immediately reduce the temperature to 190°C/fan 170°C/375°F/gas mark 5 and roast the chicken for about 35 minutes, basting with the juices now and then, until deeply golden; 10 minutes before the end of cooking, sprinkle the sesame seeds over the skin.

Serve warm if you're planning to eat at home, otherwise skim off any visible fat by tilting the pan, then keep basting with the juices as the chicken cools. Chill thoroughly and eat within 48 hours, with Georgina's Toasted Couscous with Green Leaves (see right).

GEORGINA'S TOASTED COUSCOUS WITH GREEN LEAVES

MY DEAR FRIEND GEORGINA AND I MET AT COOKERY SCHOOL and have been partners in crime ever since. Among other things, Georgina champions a winning way with Israeli (giant) or standard couscous that may be adapted to most grains and grain-like ingredients, think quinoa, millet, spelt, barley... the list goes on. Before simmering, you toast them in a frying pan with a little oil and/or butter, stirring often. Once golden and fragrant, the nuttiness of each grain will be amplified, lending an added resonance. Unless you are a vegetarian and are making this separately, pack the chicken in the same box as the couscous, so the chicken juices add to and sweeten the dressing. Transport the leaves separately, or lay on top of the chicken and couscous, only mixing in when you eat, to keep them sprightly.

Heat 1 tbsp of the oil in a large frying pan and add the couscous. Toast over a medium-high heat, stirring often, until it turns a deep golden brown and smells toasted.

Cover the couscous with water – you'll need about 675ml - add a pinch of salt and bring to the boil. Simmer, stirring often, for about 14 minutes, until all the water has been absorbed. Remove from the heat and allow to cool.

Stir in the remaining oil, the lemon zest and juice, herbs and spring onions. Season to taste and eat with the cardamom chicken thighs and a pile of the green leaves, folding them into the chicken juices and the couscous to dress as you eat.

SERVES 4
PREP 15 MINUTES
COOK ABOUT 15 MINUTES

3 tbsp olive oil

220g Israeli (giant) or standard couscous

finely grated zest of 1 unwaxed lemon and a squeeze of juice

large handful each of mint and parsley leaves, finely chopped

4 spring onions, very finely chopped

2 handfuls of mixed leaves, such as rocket, watercress, young sorrel or baby spinach

BEACH CRICKET BARBECUE FOR 6

BROWN BUTTER DABS | A PICNIC POTATO SALAD | *Pickled red onion and cucumber salad* | BLUEBERRY, ALMOND AND VANILLA CHOUX BUNS

Frying local fish on a fire; playing ragtaggle ball games; sipping an honest – and not in the least bit fancy – cocktail as the light fades... the most memorable summer days are made of this.

Setting up a base camp, however, with just a few rustic luxuries, adds to the occasion greatly. The extent of your beach barbecue paraphernalia will depend very much upon location; hamper of food and drink aside, a sturdy frying pan, matches and a rug to sit on are all that's needed for the most basic beach supper. Perhaps a cricket bat and ball, too. Firewood – and even fish – the beach and sea can provide.

First off, finding out if it's legal to build a fire on the beach you've chosen is pretty vital. Of course, there are usually signs about that will let you know, in no uncertain terms. If you're lucky enough to be able to build a fire, as always, leave everything as you found it. That means dousing fires with water or wet sand and taking rubbish away with you.

When it comes to the menu, most of it can be prepared in advance. The fish will need sizzling and the choux buns are best filled on site, but that's about the size of it. Both the salads won't mind being made that morning, along with the vanilla cream for the buns.

Nostalgic soft drinks are a must. Tuck them into a bucket of ice. I also have a weakness for simple cocktails shaken in glass jars. Pop your chosen ingredients, say, for a gin and tonic – a wedge of fresh lime (squeezed in), ice and gin – in a jam jar, screw on the lid and shake vigorously. Top up with as much tonic as you want and plunge a straw in.

Beach cricket, rock pooling, sunbathing, paddling and swimming should keep everybody happily occupied and, with any luck, there'll still be a few cubes of ice left for that drink once the sun goes down.

BROWN BUTTER DABS

SERVES 6
PREP VERY LITTLE
COOK AROUND 6 MINUTES PER
    PAIR OF DABS

about 6 very fresh dabs
    assuming 1 per person, more if
    the fish are smaller than about
    400g each
3 small pots (about 60g each) of
    brown potted shrimps
lemons, a squeeze of juice and
    wedges to serve
a little chopped parsley (optional)

MY FAMILY IS LUCKY ENOUGH TO OWN A LITTLE BOLTHOLE BY THE SEA. The beach is a quiet beauty; perfect for those impromptu cricket and Frisbee games and a spot of meandering rock pooling, once the tide sweeps out. Fittingly, we shot the accompanying photographs there.

Nearby Rye houses a fleet of fishing boats and the fish for sale is some of the best and freshest I've seen. The underused dab, a native flatfish similar to plaice, I suppose, but much smaller, is impressively good value and delicious. Give me a delicate dab or two rather than a slab of imported tuna any day.

Potted shrimps, already beautifully spiced and set in clarified butter, are a great boon for the outdoor cook here. If you forget the parsley, and I frequently do, all you need take to the beach are the shrimp pots, dabs, lemons and seasoning.

Make a neat slit on the white belly side of the dabs – you're looking for the soft spot just below the head – and remove the guts. This shouldn't be a messy job. Rinse well.

You'll need a heavy-based pan to cook the fish, preferably one that will hold a couple of dabs at a time. Balance the pan safely over a hot flame, assuming the heat source is a campfire, and add the butter from the top of a shrimp pot. It should sizzle briskly.

Add two fish, brown-sides down, and fry until golden and crisp. Add all the potted shrimps from the pot and their remaining butter and turn the fish over. Again, cook until the fish is turning golden. Remove from the heat, shower with lemon juice, salt and pepper and, should you have it, a little chopped parsley. Serve sharpish and get on with cooking the remaining fish in the same way.

BASIC RULES & GUIDELINES
of beach cricket

YOU'LL NEED QUITE A BIT OF SPACE FOR STARTERS; this isn't one for crowded beaches. Mark out a line in the sand for the bowler to start from and the batsman to run to. The other essentials are stumps of some sort (two or three vertical sticks at about thigh-height with a little stick balanced horizontally on top. Driftwood is a good source), a bat and at least one ball. Improvise as needed.

EVERYBODY IS IN PLAY AT ALL TIMES.

No sitting on the sidelines waiting to bat. Divide into teams if you must but every player, no matter which side they are on, has to put maximum effort into fielding.

EACH 'OVER' USUALLY CONSISTS OF SIX BALLS,

bowled at the wicket by the bowler. The batsman tries to hit each ball as far as he can, or in a way that will enable him to run to the marked bowling line from the wicket – and back – before the ball is returned to the bowler or thrown at the wicket. Each length of the pitch is a 'run' and the tip of the bat must tap the ground at the end for it to qualify. When returning to the wicket, the batsman must shout 'IN!'. The aim is to get as many runs as possible.

Main ways to get the batsman
out: catch the batted ball before it has hit the ground. Throw the ball at the wicket and dislodge the little stick on top while the batsman is away from it. Bowl to hit the wicket, dislodging the little stick.

IT IS UP TO THE PLAYERS TO DECIDE HOW MANY OVERS THE GAME WILL BE ON THE DAY.

If no-one can be bothered to keep count, the bowler has a right to bowl two more balls from the time somebody questions whether the over has been played or not.

HAVE A GOOD SUPPLY OF TENNIS BALLS AT THE READY.

Nothing top-of-the-range mind, you're bound to lose the odd one to a watery grave.

PARENTS AND GRANDPARENTS ARE NOT ALLOWED TO UMPIRE unless they swear to be utterly fair and non-biased for or against offspring. If no agreement can be reached on a decision, a compromise must be reached. If no compromise can be found, the 'last man standing' rule applies: first team to leave the playing area forfeits the wicket. That includes getting in the sea.

Dogs do count as fielders,
but only if they return the ball on command. Running off with it does not count. The dog is on the same side as his or her owner, or nearest relative of the owner. If a ball hits a dog, however, the batsman is immediately out and must apologise profusely.

TO QUALIFY AS A NO BALL, the ball has to hit the ground a good person's length in front of the batsman.

A BATSMAN CANNOT BOWL STRAIGHT AWAY IF HE HAS JUST BEEN GIVEN OUT.

TO QUALIFY AS A WIDE, the ball has to be thrown further to one side than the batsman can reach at full extension.

Unless they are particularly good at cricket,
it is usual to give children first ball's grace, at least until they get their eye in.

IF A BATSMAN MISSES three consecutive (good) balls, he is declared out.

If nobody can be bothered to keep score
at all, the winner is the player deemed to have shown the most sporting prowess. Assuming this sporting prowess runs to swimming and/or paddling, the winner should always be thrown in the sea by the other players.

A PICNIC POTATO SALAD

I FAVOUR PINK FIR APPLE HERE AS THE SPUD OF CHOICE; it's nutty, waxy and soaks up a dressing quite beautifully when warm. Knobbly it is too, but that's hardly a disadvantage.

The trick, and there is only one – this is just a (very good) potato salad after all – is to get everything chopped and prepped while the potatoes simmer away. As soon as the spuds are drained, douse them in the dressing. There will be a generous amount, allowing for a fair bit to soak in. Serve just-warm or cool.

Simmer the potatoes in salted boiling water for 18-20 minutes, or until tender, as this will depend greatly on size. While they are cooking, whisk the oil, vinegar, mustard and sugar together. Season generously with salt and pepper. Taste and adjust as you like; the dressing should be feisty.

Drain the potatoes well, tip into a bowl and add the dressing. Mix well, then fold in the spring onions and herbs, reserving the cress. Leave until warm or completely cool, turning the potatoes over occasionally. Tumble the mustard cress through just before serving.

SERVES 6
PREP 15 MINUTES
COOK ABOUT 20 MINUTES, PLUS COOLING

1kg new potatoes, a waxy variety that actually tastes of something, halved if large
75ml extra virgin olive oil
3 tbsp good red wine vinegar, or any quality vinegar you fancy
1 tbsp wholegrain mustard
pinch of caster sugar
1 bunch of spring onions, trimmed and sliced
small bunch of chives, snipped
handful of tarragon leaves, chopped
handful of snipped mustard cress

PICKLED RED ONION AND CUCUMBER SALAD

QUICK PICKLING FOR BEGINNERS. Granted, this becomes more of a piquant salad, but the onion makes a mild introduction to the addictive world of pickles...

Warm the sugar, salt and vinegar with a splash of water over a very low heat, stirring until just dissolved. Leave to cool, then add the onion, mix well and set aside for at least 15 minutes or up to an hour. More if you like. The onions will mellow and lighten in colour prettily, turning their pickling liquid to a blushing pink.

Add the remaining ingredients and a grind of pepper; it shouldn't need any salt but taste and adjust as you like.

SERVES 6
PREP 20 MINUTES, PLUS STEEPING

2½ tbsp unrefined caster sugar
large pinch of salt
75ml red wine vinegar
2 small red onions, halved and very finely sliced
½ large cucumber, peeled, halved, deseeded and sliced
a few radishes, trimmed, scrubbed and finely sliced
small handful of mint leaves, torn
a handful of radish sprouts

BLUEBERRY, ALMOND AND VANILLA CHOUX BUNS

I ORIGINALLY WANTED TO FINISH THIS MENU WITH A BIG PARIS BREST – one of those enormous choux pastry rings, scattered with almonds and fit to burst with pastry cream and non-traditional blueberries – but the logistics of transporting it to the beach, let alone eating it, inspired a re-think. Manageable little buns encrusted with golden almonds can be filled just about anywhere and are easy to carry when still un-filled.

    Once cooked and cooled, the buns can be frozen if it makes life easier. Open-freeze, spaced out on trays, then, once hard, transfer to freezer bags, seal well and keep for up to two months. Defrost and re-crisp in a low oven before halving and filling as below.

MAKES ABOUT 20
PREP 20–30 MINUTES
COOK 20–30 MINUTES

FOR THE CHOUX PASTRY
105g plain flour
pinch of fine salt
85g unsalted butter, diced
3 eggs, lightly beaten
75g flaked almonds

This is the way I was taught to make choux pastry at cookery school. Fold a large piece of paper (greaseproof will do) in half and open back out again. The fold will be your flour chute. Sift the flour a couple of times, add the salt and pour on to the paper.

Preheat the oven to 190°C/fan 170°C/375°F/gas mark 5. Put the butter and 200ml water in a saucepan and set over a low-ish heat to melt the butter. As soon as the butter has melted, increase the heat to high so the liquid reaches a fierce boil as quickly as possible.

Immediately tip the flour down its paper chute into the boiling liquid. Remove from the heat and beat vigorously with a wooden spoon. As soon as the mixture looks smooth and comes away from the sides of the pan, stop beating. Otherwise it will become greasy. Spread out on a plate to cool quickly. When cool enough to touch comfortably, transfer to a mixing bowl and, using a handheld whisk, beat in the egg, a little at a time. You may not need it all, so only keep adding until a scoop of the choux drops reluctantly from its spoon when jerked sharply.

Fit a pastry bag with a large, plain nozzle and fill with the choux. To make this easier with only two hands, balance the open pastry bag in a pint glass, folding the excess fabric over the top as you spoon the pastry in.

Line one large, or two smaller, baking sheets with non-stick baking parchment and scatter with half the flaked almonds.

CONT...

Pipe (or spoon, if you don't have a piping bag) large walnut-sized balls on to the baking sheet(s) in rows, allowing space for the buns-to-be to rise. Sprinkle with the remaining almonds and bake for about 30 minutes until puffed, crisp and deeply golden. Check after 20 minutes and reduce the oven temperature slightly if the almonds are browning too much. After 30 minutes, turn the oven off, prop the door open slightly and leave the buns inside for a further 15 minutes to dry out. Cool on wire racks. It's best to use them immediately for ultimate crispness, but the empty buns can be stored for a day or two in an airtight tin.

Make the vanilla cream filling. Scrape the seeds from the vanilla pod with a small knife. In a large bowl, whisk the cream, crème fraîche, vanilla seeds, icing sugar and vanilla extract (if using) together until firm enough to hold its shape.

With a serrated knife, slice each choux bun in half horizontally. Heap a generous spoonful of vanilla cream on to each lower half and top with a few blueberries. Replace the top halves and, if you feel inclined, dust with icing sugar. Eat soon, before they have a chance to soften too much, with the extra blueberries.

FOR THE VANILLA CREAM

1 plump vanilla pod, split
     lengthways
200ml double cream
200ml crème fraîche
100g icing sugar, sifted, plus
     more to dust
a small dash of vanilla extract
     (optional)
400g blueberries

Rockpools

With a bit of luck, these magical windows into the sea will house a teeming variety of sea life. Try to disturb the pools as little as possible as you look and go gently; don't force or break anything. If you have any children with you, they will adore clambering over the rocks at low tide. Take a small net for scooping and have a bucket of sea water ready to keep any tiny fish or shrimp in while you look at them. Be sure to return any creatures and leave everything as you found it.

What you might see under and around the water...

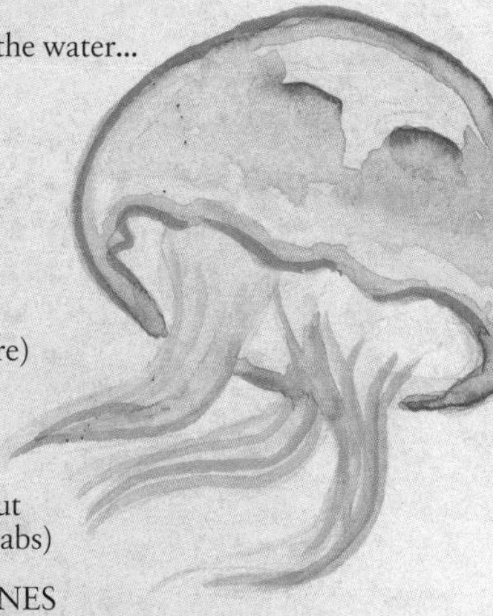

SHRIMP

JELLYFISH
(moon, lion's mane, blue, bluefire)

MUSSELS

CRABS
(most commonly shore crabs but
also porcelain crabs and hermit crabs)

CUTTLEFISH and CUTTLEBONES
(collect them for budgies)

RAZOR SHELLS
(ensis ensis)

GOBY
(common or rock)

STARFISH

TUBE WORMS

PERIWINKLES, LIMPETS
and BARNACLES

ANEMONES
(green, strawberry, brown or red forms).
Seen either in 'bead' (closed) or open

SEAWEEDS
(lava, dulce, Irish moss or caragen)

A CHIC, EASY PICNIC FOR 10

AUTUMNAL PANZANELLA | GRIDDLED AUBERGINES AND SUMMER SQUASH | *Brik with a roast tomato sauce* SESAME BISCUITS WITH ICED WATERMELON

Loved by most, who will be on board with me regarding picnics, but loathed by a notable few, lugging your lunch to that elusive, perfect spot really is worth it. I promise. As long as the heavens don't open... This is definitely a time to watch the forecast closely and, if the weather fails, there's always a picnic blanket on the living room floor to fall back on. At least then you'll be able to eat with proper cutlery, which should please the naysayers.

Guesstimating serving sizes for a large picnic is a precarious game, balancing those content to sit nicely and eat with others who will be more interested in playing Frisbee and dashing about. I work on the premise that one of these main course or hefty salad recipes will serve at least eight, but the whole menu below would actually stretch to 10.

Pack your bounty in Tupperware or light bowls, cling filmed securely. Take lots of napkins and a good, thick blanket. Any dressings or sauces should be carried separately, in lidded jam jars, if adding them too early would result in soggy salads.

Pro-picnickers, of which I am most certainly one, will know that eating out of doors is magical when you get it right. Granted, the holy grail of locations are mountain tops, forests, fields and lake sides, but some of my best have been in back gardens and parks.

Every year, my friend Tab, who styled the pictures in this book, has a birthday picnic in a secret park in London. She sets up a corner with lovely old bunting and tea lights strung through the trees and everyone brings a dish. Groups of friends turn up through the day and sit on blankets eating, chatting and occasionally kicking a ball. With just a little effort, she creates something magical. By dusk, the children have gone home and mojitos and birthday cake have appeared for the big kids who remain.

AUTUMNAL PANZANELLA

**SERVES 8–10, AS PART OF A
  PICNIC SPREAD**
PREP 30 MINUTES
COOK 40 MINUTES

FOR THE SALAD

6 tbsp olive oil (ideally from the
  artichoke jar), plus more for
  the roasting tins
300g ripe, smallish tomatoes,
  halved
2 tbsp red wine vinegar
2 red onions, halved and thickly
  sliced through the root
4 mixed red and yellow Romano
  peppers, cut into rough pieces
½ large loaf of day-old
  sourdough, cut into 3cm cubes
1 fat garlic clove, crushed
400g grilled artichokes in oil,
  drained weight
1 large bunch of basil

FOR THE DRESSING

1 fat garlic clove, crushed
4 tbsp red wine vinegar
pinch of caster sugar
6 tbsp extra virgin olive oil
2 heaped tbsp capers, rinsed well
  and drained

IF YOU'RE IN THE MARKET FOR SPLASHING OUT, it's well worth getting hold of some of those pricey grilled artichoke hearts in oil; one up on the typical antipasti type in jars. Find them in Italian delis or in Waitrose, which does some very nice Apulian ones. Panzanella benefits from being made a few hours ahead, allowing the bread to soak up the dressing and tomato juices. Take the basil leaves along as a bunch, tearing or slicing the leaves into the salad at the picnic spot.

Preheat the oven to 180°C/fan 160°C/350°F/gas mark 4. Lightly oil a couple of large roasting tins. Arrange the tomatoes in one, cut-sides up, and drizzle with the red wine vinegar, 2 tbsp oil and salt and pepper. Toss the red onions, peppers and 2 tbsp oil in the other roasting tin. Roast both tins for 35-40 minutes, stirring the peppers and onions every now and then but leaving the tomatoes alone. All should be soft and beginning to char at the edges. Set aside to cool.

Meanwhile, toss the bread with the remaining olive oil and the garlic. Season and roast in the oven for about 15 minutes, turning at least once, until pale golden and crisp. Again, set aside to cool.

Combine the dressing ingredients and season to taste, going easy on the salt because of the capers.

At least 30 minutes, or up to eight hours, before eating, toss everything together: the peppers and onions, tomatoes, toasted bread, artichokes and dressing. Don't be gentle, the juices from the roast vegetables need to mingle with the dressing. Add the shredded or torn basil leaves 10 minutes or so before serving and toss again.

GRIDDLED AUBERGINES AND SUMMER SQUASH

TIME SPENT PEERING OVER THE GRIDDLE PAN, TONGS AT THE READY, IS INEVITABLE HERE. Griddling thinly sliced vegetables takes a while, simply because there are always so darned many paper-thin slices to cook. Two griddle pans would be the ideal but unrealistic so, failing that, work in batches and be patient. The good news is that all this can be done well ahead of time and smoky ribbons of own-griddled courgettes and aubergines will a truly stunning salad make.

You can dress this on site (in which case, carry the dressing in a lidded jam jar), or a short while beforehand; take the mozzarella and bunch of mint along separately, ready to add at the last minute.

Start by slicing the courgettes and aubergines lengthways with a sharp knife, ideally 2-3mm thick. A sharp swivel peeler works well for the courgettes. Toss the sliced vegetables with the olive oil and season generously.

Place a dry griddle pan over a high heat for a few minutes, until smoking hot. Working in small batches, lay vegetable slices out in a single layer, only turning each slice over with tongs when well-marked with dark griddle lines (about a minute on each side). As they are ready (when they are marked on both sides), transfer the vegetables to a bowl and continue cooking the rest. If you want to keep the cooled vegetables overnight before making the salad, toss them with a little extra virgin olive oil before covering and chilling.

To make the dressing, toast the coriander seeds in a dry pan for a minute, until fragrant. Crush lightly in a mortar and pestle or with the underside of a cup. Combine the crushed seeds with the chilli flakes, honey, lemon zest and juice, extra virgin olive oil and seasoning to taste.

No more than two hours, or up to a few minutes, before serving, toss the griddled vegetables with the dressing. Just before eating, toss through the mozzarella and the mint.

SERVES 8 AS PART OF A PICNIC SPREAD
PREP 20 MINUTES
COOK 20 MINUTES

FOR THE SALAD
4 courgettes, trimmed
2 large aubergines, trimmed
4 tbsp olive oil
2 balls buffalo mozzarella, drained and sliced or torn into pieces
1 small bunch of mint, leaves picked and shredded or torn if large

FOR THE DRESSING
1½ tbsp coriander seeds
good pinch of chilli flakes
1 tbsp runny honey
finely grated zest and juice of 1 unwaxed lemon
4 tbsp, or more, extra virgin olive oil

HOW SWEET TO BE A CLOUD, FLOATING IN THE BLUE...

Streaky groups of **cirrocumulus**, white and high in the sky, imply the weather will set fair.

Sheets of **cirrostratus** clouds cover the whole sky, only allowing a faint glow of sun or moon to shine through. Cirrostratus usually mean drizzle or even rain will arrive the next day.

Thin and wispy white **cirrus** clouds indicate the weather will stay fair for now, but a change is on its way.

HIGH (5,000–12,000 metres)

Fluffy blankets of grey-white **altocumulus** block out the sun when they pass over it, causing dramatic light and dark effects. A thunderstorm is likely to arrive in a few hours.

Grey or blue-grey **altostratus** block out the sun and the whole sky. A storm is coming...

MIDDLE (2,000–8,000 metres)

Stratus, the drizzle clouds, look like suspended greyish fog. If it is cold enough, the drizzle will fall as light snow.

Cumulonimbus are said to look like giant anvils. The ends of the anvil can point to a rainstorm in the offing.

Beautiful **stratocumulus** lie low in the sky in rows and clumps like herds of fluffy grey sheep. Like sheep they are rather benign; stratocumulus do not bring wet weather with them, but rain could hit when they meet another weather front.

LOW (below 2,000 metres)

Fluffy **cumulus** float over blue skies like clumps of white candyfloss. They bring fair weather but, if a cumulus starts to grow upwards, keep an eye on things; it might get windy and wet later.

Nimbostratus sits in grumpy light grey sheets. Time to sing 'rain, rain, go away, come again another day'.

VERTICAL (low bases from 5,000 metres and very high tops reaching as high as 15,000 metres)

BRIK
WITH A ROAST TOMATO SAUCE

MAKES 10 OF EACH TYPE
PREP 40 MINUTES PER BATCH
    OF 10
COOK 1 HOUR 20 MINUTES
    (FETA FILLING) – 1¾ HOURS
    (LAMB FILLING)

FOR THE LAMB FILLING
550g lamb neck, trimmed of
    excess fat and cut into
    5cm pieces
1 large onion, chopped
1 tbsp olive oil
300g unpeeled, waxy potatoes,
    cut into 1-2cm cubes
1 tsp cumin seeds
1 ½ tbsp capers
large handful of chopped parsley

FOR THE FETA FILLING
2 tbsp olive oil
1 large red onion, diced
300g unpeeled, waxy potatoes,
    cut into 1-2cm cubes
1 tsp cumin seeds
250g spinach, washed and any
    coarse stalks removed
100g feta, crumbled
½ tbsp capers
large handful of chopped parsley
no salt!

FOR THE BRIKS
10 tbsp olive oil
4 eggs, lightly beaten
20 brik pastry sheets

BRIK, A CLOSE COUSIN OF THE BÖREK, boureki, bourekas, byrek, and burek (I could go on...), is rooted in Algeria and Tunisia. As you can imagine, there are myriad variations, but the main premise of fried or baked pastry enclosing a filling remains true. Traditionally, each brik is fried to order in hot oil until crisp. Gossamer-fine pastry is wrapped around a simple raw filling, including a fresh egg dropped into the centre before sealing. The challenge with picnic food lies in the sitting about; sogginess and greasiness is unwelcome and that often means fried foods will be sub-optimal by the time you come to eat them. In my, cheerfully inauthentic, version, an egg and olive oil glaze turns the pastry crisp and golden and that crisp quality should hold for a good few hours. Enough time to reach your picnic spot and eat in the sun. I'd encourage you to crack a small egg into each pastry just before wrapping if you like the idea. I do and enjoyed the spoils very much when recipe testing but, in the end, the egg got dropped because more of my willing testers plumped for the eggless version. I settled on two fillings, one slow-cooked lamb, suitable for the sharper air of September and, for vegetarians, a feta and spinach version. Both have the bolster of waxy potatoes with capers and cumin to brighten. Play around with them. One of my favourites is a simple mix of diced (raw) red onion, crab and caper. Brik pastry is available in Turkish shops and larger Waitrose stores but, if it isn't forthcoming, use filo. I daresay the fillings would work a charm in a shortcrust or puff pastry wrapper too.

Preheat the oven to 160°C/fan 140°C/325°F/gas mark 3. For the lamb filling, combine all the ingredients except the capers and parsley in a small roasting tin, season, cover tightly with foil and cook for 1½ hours or so, until incredibly tender. A fork should meet no real resistance when you use it to roughly shred the lamb. Let cool, stir in the capers and parsley and adjust the seasoning to taste.

For the vegetarian filling, combine the olive oil, onion, potato and cumin seeds in a small roasting tin or dish. Cover tightly with foil and roast for one hour, at the same temperature as the lamb, until the potatoes are tender. Immediately stir in the spinach and re-cover with foil. Return to the oven for three to five minutes to wilt the spinach, stir in the remaining ingredients, and set aside to cool.

The fillings may be made up to two days in advance and kept chilled. Bring up to room temperature before using.

CONT...

When ready to finish the briks, preheat the oven to 180°C/fan 160°C/350°F/gas mark 4. Line four large baking sheets with non-stick baking parchment. Whisk the olive oil with the eggs and 2 tbsp water in a bowl; have a pastry brush at the ready.

Lay a sheet of pastry on a work surface, peeling it from its paper backing. Brush lightly with the egg mixture, then lay a heaped tablespoon of your chosen filling in the top right of the circle. Fold the pastry over in half and then again into a quarter to enclose the filling. Brush more egg over the edges and outside, to seal and glaze. Space the briks out on the baking sheets, keeping the side where the filling is more visible facing upwards. This is to ensure that the underside crisps up, protected as it is by an extra couple of pastry layers. Repeat to make 10 briks of each type. Bake for about 15 minutes, until golden and crisp-edged.

Cool on the baking sheets, then pack carefully in layers of greaseproof paper. Transport the sauce (below) in a separate pot.

ROAST TOMATO SAUCE

MAKES ENOUGH FOR 8 WITH THE BRIKS
PREP 10 MINUTES
COOK 1 HOUR

1kg ripe tomatoes, halved
pinch of caster sugar
good drizzle of extra virgin olive oil

THE PANZANELLA RECIPE IN THIS CHAPTER already features roast tomatoes, cooked at a higher temperature and for less time, but gluts are there to be taken advantage of and this blueprint sauce is endlessly versatile, ready to be altered as you wish. The long and gentle roasting concentrates the tomato's late-summer flavour enough for it to shine unadorned, but should you wish to enhance it, try whole garlic cloves – added to the roasting tin with their skins on – to be squeezed in after cooking. Herbs such as thyme, oregano and rosemary torn in beforehand will add depth, as will cumin and coriander seeds, chilli, smoked paprika and even chipotle chillies. Instead of crushing it, purée the sauce if you like, with or without basil or mint. The tomato skins may be removed after cooking for a more refined finish.

Preheat the oven to 150°C/fan 130°C/300°F/gas mark 2. Sit the tomato halves snugly in a roasting tin, cut sides up. Scatter the sugar over with salt and pepper, drizzle generously with olive oil and roast for one hour, until the tomatoes have shrivelled slightly. Use a fork or a potato masher to crush the tomatoes down, forming a rustic sauce. Keep, chilled, for up to five days. Pack into lidded pots and use as a sauce for the briks (see page 114 and above).

HOW TO
forage for razor clams

FINDING THE CLAMS...

When there's a full moon and a new moon, tides sweep out faster and further, exposing swathes of hidden sandy beach that go unseen at other times of the month. Razor clams live around the point of low tide, so larger tides expose their breathing holes and make harvesting far more easy. There are two particularly low tides in the UK, one falls in mid-March and the other in mid-September. If at all possible, go clamming when these tides fall; your chances of success will be at their highest.

Look the tide times up and go to the beach when the tide is almost at its lowest. Take a tub of fine salt, the everyday 'table' sort with a small dispenser in the top. Step quietly and leave the dog at home; the clams will quickly retract if they sense a disturbance.

RAZOR SHELLS *(ensis ensis), or razor clams, or razor fish, are sand-burrowing bivalves. They grow to 12-20cm long and, with their curved, brownish shells, resemble an old barber's blade, hence the name. If you can get to a beach that is sandy at low tide, it is so worth foraging for razor clams; they are as delightful as any scallop and it's fun.*

Working along the sand near to the water, look for the breathing holes which will be smaller than a 10 pence piece and elongated rather than round. Sometimes the holes will 'foam' as the clam breathes. Pour salt into the hole and wait for a few seconds. The clam should push up to the surface because he thinks the briny tide is coming in. Be patient and wait until he is exposed by at least a thumb's length before you strike. Grasp the clam and pull firmly but slowly, easing it from the sand.

As you go, put the clams into a bucket of clean sea water to help purge any sand out. Don't keep them in this water for longer than an hour or so though, or they might drown.

If you buy your clams from a fishmonger, they will be cleaned already. Make sure they smell pleasantly of the sea, rather than at all fishy, and that the flesh is whitish and plump, not discoloured with brownish tinges.

...AND PREPARING THEM

Like squid, clams are easy to overcook, so go cautiously to get the best from their sweet flesh. Eat as soon as you can, but they keep overnight, wrapped in wet newspaper and well-chilled.

The possibilities are varied and if you're looking for something different, razor clams make a beautiful ceviche. Three or four each will do as a starter, six to eight as a main course. The easiest way for novices to prepare them is:

Soak in cool, unsalted water for 30 minutes, then rinse. This is to remove as much sand as possible. Grill or steam in their shells for a minute or so, just enough to open them. Leave to cool a little before taking the flesh out and cutting off the digger (the black end). If the clams look sandy, rinse again. In bad cases, you can snip along the length of the clam, rinsing sand away as you go.

To grill them (the simplest way), return them to the shells and grill until firm and just opaque.

Serve with garlic butter, or sizzled chorizo and its oil with parsley. Vietnamese-style dressings of fish sauce, sugar, lime juice and finely chopped chilli, spooned over the steamed flesh, are also excellent.

You can also treat the razor clams like mussels, adding them to a buttery mix of softened shallot and garlic, then pouring in white wine and covering until cooked. Chopped parsley and an optional slick of cream will top things off nicely.

SESAME BISCUITS WITH ICED WATERMELON

MAKES AROUND 25 BISCUITS
PREP 20 MINUTES
COOK 12 MINUTES

110g unsalted butter, softened
150g light or dark brown
    soft sugar
1 egg
8 tbsp light tahini paste
1 tsp vanilla extract
pinch of salt
200g plain flour
1 tsp bicarbonate of soda
50g sesame seeds
30g demerara sugar

THE ICED WATERMELON INVOLVES NOTHING MORE FANCY THAN A BOWLING BALL-SIZED, whole watermelon, thoroughly chilled overnight. Take a knife and a bag of ice along to sit the sliced melon on, stealing a few cubes to keep drinks cool. Soft-crumbed biscuits are a lovely way to use up the jar of tahini that sits around between sporadic bouts of houmous-making. Use 15g less butter and add a tablespoon of toasted sesame oil in its place if you particularly love sesame. Dark brown sugar will garner moodier results than light. I have also had much success substituting peanut butter for the tahini and finely chopped peanuts for sesame seeds, so I'm quite sure any nut butter and its matching nut would work too. Lastly on the variation advice, ground ginger and/or cinnamon make warming additions in the colder months.

Preheat the oven to 180°C/fan 160°C/350°F/gas mark 4. Line two large baking sheets with non-stick baking parchment.

Using electric beaters, or a wooden spoon and elbow grease, beat the butter and sugar together until light, followed by the egg. Follow with the tahini, a tablespoon at a time as you beat, then the vanilla extract and salt.

Sift the flour and bicarbonate of soda over, followed by a tablespoon of the sesame seeds, and mix with a wooden spoon until combined.

Empty the remaining sesame seeds on to a plate with the demerara sugar. Roll heaped teaspoons of the dough into spheres, then roll these firmly in the sesame-sugar plate. Space well apart on the baking sheets and cook for 10-12 minutes, until pale golden. Leave to firm up on the baking sheets for a couple of minutes, then transfer to wire racks to cool completely.

HARVEST FESTIVAL LUNCH FOR 8

CRISP HAM HOCK AND PUMPKIN SALAD, CHILLI DRESSING AND TOASTED PUMPKIN SEEDS
CHICKEN AND WILD MUSHROOM PIES, BUTTERED KALE | *Black grape jelly with muscat sabayon*

If there was ever a time to shop at farmers' markets, farm shops and local greengrocers, this is the season to do it. Mid- to late-autumn's produce stalls spill forth with ruddy, russet-skinned fruits and tactile gourds. It is now, rather than amid spring's deluge of new growth, that the soil and the changing seasons can be felt most keenly. Cooking for large numbers is easy when there is so much good – and cheap – bounty to be found. And we are spoilt for choice. From Jerusalem artichokes, wild mushrooms and truffles to perfumed grapes in dripping bunches and the last of the buxom figs, splitting under their own weight, a need to harvest, to stock up for the cold to come, looms large.

All of a sudden, it is OK to spend a weekend afternoon pottering in the kitchen, making a stew for later or baking a cake. Earlier in the autumn – and especially during a late Indian summer – it feels like a waste of summer's remnants to spend any more time indoors than is necessary. The arrival of cold mornings and dark evenings bring with them a twinge of sad relief. Summer is done with for another year and winter creeps in to take her place.

A warming, late lunch is ideal for an autumnal weekend. Hopefully, the day will be suited to a golden morning walk through turning leaves and conkers. Thankfully, a chicken pie will be just as welcome on grey-skied and damp days which, given our climate, is the far more likely scenario. The recipes should allow time off for good behaviour, for much can be made in advance. The grape jellies and their sabayon, the components of the salad and the chicken pies can all be done a day, or two days, ahead. The morning's cooking should then consist of mere assembly jobs: re-warming the ham for the salad before jumbling everything together to eat; baking the pies; and wilting a mound of buttery greens.

CRISP HAM HOCK AND PUMPKIN SALAD,
CHILLI DRESSING AND TOASTED PUMPKIN SEEDS

SERVES 8
PREP 40 MINUTES
COOK 2 HOURS 50 MINUTES

THIS RAMBUNCTIOUS SALAD happens to be one of my very favourite recipes in the book. Normally, I try to take the authentic route with Asian dishes, but mild olive oil and pumpkin seeds make for such a harmonious marriage with chilli, ginger and kaffir lime that, in this case, I don't think authenticity matters a jot.

All too often, ham is cured in overly salty brines. Remedy this by soaking the hocks in cool water for a few hours before cooking, changing the water as and when you remember.

Preheat the oven to 160°C/fan 140°C/325°F/gas mark 3. Put the ham hocks in a small roasting tin and cover with foil. Cook for two hours or so, until almost falling apart. Cool until you can strip away the fat and skin, tearing the meat into large pieces. (This may be done up to two days in advance. Return to room temperature for 15 minutes or so, then place in a roasting tin, cover with foil and re-heat in a low oven.) Increase the oven temperature to 220°C/fan 200°C/425°F/gas mark 7. Toss the pumpkin with the oil, season generously and roast on a lined baking sheet for about 30 minutes, until golden at the edges and tender. Leave to cool slightly. (Again, this can be done up to two days beforehand. Return to room temperature before using.)

On to the dressing. To prepare the lime leaves, stack them on top of each other and roll up tightly. Slice very, very finely to get whisper-thin shreds, avoiding the stalk (chuck that bit away). Place 4 tbsp of the oil in a frying pan and add the shallots. Cook gently, stirring often, for about 10 minutes. They should look shrivelled but not deeply coloured. Now add the sugar and stir for two minutes. Follow with the chillies, ginger, garlic, lemon grass and lime leaves, keeping the heat very low and cooking for a further five minutes. Remove from the heat and leave to cool slightly. Stir in the soy sauce, lime juice, remaining olive oil and the sesame oil.

Toast the pumpkin seeds in a dry frying pan, shaking them about until puffed and fragrant. Set aside to cool. To serve, combine the salad and herb leaves in a large bowl, scatter the pumpkin, avocado and ham over, followed by the dressing and a twist of black pepper. Fluff everything up a bit and shower with pumpkin seeds. Take to the table for everyone to serve themselves.

FOR THE SALAD
3 smoked ham hocks
900g pumpkin or squash, peeled if the skin is very tough, and sliced 2-3cm thick
2 tbsp olive oil
100g pumpkin seeds
2 large handfuls of characterful mixed leaves (mizuna, rocket, chard, young spinach)
generous handful of coriander leaves
handful of Thai basil leaves (or more coriander if you can't find it)
2 large, ripe avocados, cut into thin segments

FOR THE DRESSING
4 kaffir lime leaves
6 tbsp mild olive oil
3 shallots, very finely sliced
45g palm sugar or 3 tbsp light brown sugar
2 red chillies, very finely sliced
thumb-sized piece of fresh root ginger, peeled and sliced into fine matchsticks
1 fat garlic clove, finely chopped
2 lemon grass stalks, trimmed and finely sliced
3 tbsp soy sauce
juice of 1 lime
1 tsp toasted sesame oil

CHICKEN AND WILD MUSHROOM PIES,
BUTTERED KALE

**MAKES 8 INDIVIDUAL PIES,
OR 2 X 4-PERSON PIES**
PREP 2 HOURS
COOK ABOUT 1½ HOURS

FOR THE PASTRY
450g unsalted butter, chilled
   and cubed
950g plain flour, plus more
   to dust
2 tsp salt

FOR THE POACHED CHICKEN
1.5kg whole free-range chicken
1 large onion, halved
1 large leek, roughly chopped
2 large carrots, roughly chopped
10g dried mushrooms
bouquet garni of 2 bay leaves
   with a few sprigs of parsley
   and thyme

FOR THE FILLING
200ml white wine
150ml single cream
75g unsalted butter, cubed
75g plain flour
2 tbsp chopped parsley,
   or 1 tbsp chopped tarragon

THESE ARE PIES TO GLADDEN THE HEART. Pies of woodsy mushrooms, gently poached chicken and a sauce that really tastes of the latter, rather than of cream or stock cubes. Use eight 425ml pie dishes or ovenproof bowls, or two 20cm pie dishes for larger pies. If you can't afford wild, use chestnut and field mushrooms and give the flavour a boost with a few dried porcini, soaked and chopped.

Start by making the pastry. I find it easiest to divide the ingredients in half to make two batches; such is the life of the mass caterer... Using the pulse button, whizz half the butter, half the flour and half the salt for a couple of minutes, until it looks like coarse sand. Tip into a bowl and, using a table knife, cut in just enough iced water (around 2–3 tbsp) to get the mixture clumping together. Tip on to a work surface and lightly bring together into a ball. Flatten to form a disc and wrap in cling film. Repeat to make a second disc and chill both for at least an hour, or up to three days.

Sit the chicken, onion, leek, carrots, dried mushrooms and bouquet garni in a large casserole or saucepan; it should be snug, but not too snug, and have a bit of space above it. Cover with cool water by a couple of centimetres, then bring to the boil. Skim off any foam, then reduce the heat right, right down so the water barely sputters. Let the chicken poach for an hour, then turn the heat off and leave the bird to cool in the stock. Lift the chicken out of the stock and set aside. Skim any fat from the surface, then strain the stock. As soon it is cool enough to handle, remove the meat from the chicken, flaking it into large chunks in a mixing bowl; chucking out all the skin, fat, gristle and bones as you go.

Measure 1 litre of the strained stock into a saucepan – freeze the rest for soups and sauces – add the wine and reduce over a high heat, until only half its volume remains. Stir in the cream, taste and adjust the seasoning. Keep the liquid hot for the next stage...

To make the sauce, melt the butter in a large pan, stir in the flour and cook, stirring constantly, for a couple of minutes. Swap to a balloon whisk and slowly begin to add the hot, reduced stock, whisking constantly. Keep adding and whisking to make a thick sauce. Bring to the simmer and whisk for five minutes to get rid of any 'floury' taste. Season lightly and add the herbs.

CONT...

FOR THE MUSHROOMS

1 tbsp olive oil

15g unsalted butter

500g mixed wild mushrooms,
 brushed and torn into bits

1 fat garlic clove, crushed
 (optional)

FOR THE GLAZE

2 egg yolks, lightly beaten

2 tbsp milk

Heat the olive oil and butter for the mushrooms in your largest frying pan. Sauté the mushrooms briskly, stirring sparingly, for a few minutes, until browned in places and wilted; any liquid should have evaporated. If you are adding the garlic, throw it in a couple of minutes before removing from the heat. Season, then add to the shredded chicken. Pour the sauce over and gently mix. Cover and chill for up to 48 hours, or use straight away.

Preheat the oven to 190°C/fan 170°C/375°F/gas mark 5. Depending on the size of your oven, put one large or two medium baking trays in to preheat. Remove the pastry from the fridge about 30 minutes before needed. Cut out 16x3cm strips of baking paper or foil, two per small pie dish, laid in as a cross with the ends sticking out of the dish. This will enable you to lift the cooked pies out easily.

On a lightly floured surface, roll the first disc of pastry out to the thickness of a two pound coin. Use it to line the pie dishes (make sure the ends of the paper strips are still visible), leaving an overhang. Fill each dish with chicken, right to the top. Repeat with the second disc of pastry. Beat the egg yolk and milk together. Using a pastry brush, paint this around the rim of each pie then cut a lid and lay it over, pressing down firmly. Cut away the excess pastry and crimp the edges or press with the tines of a fork. Brush the glaze over the pies and cut a hole in the tops to release steam.

Slide them on to the preheated baking tray(s) and cook for 50 minutes to one hour, until deeply burnished. Cover them with foil if they brown too quickly. Let the cooked pies rest for a few minutes. Carefully lift from their dishes using the paper strips. (Or cut hefty slices from a large pie.) Serve with Buttered Kale (see below).

BUTTERED KALE

BUTTERED BLACK KALE WOULD BE A MORE ACCURATE TITLE, but it felt somewhat cumbersome and a touch dictatorial when there are plenty of other kales in the running.

SERVES 8
PREP 10 MINUTES
COOK 5 MINUTES OR SO

3 bunches of cavolo nero or
 other kale or greens

2 generous knobs of unsalted
 butter

dash of olive oil

2 garlic cloves, very finely sliced

good grating of nutmeg

Wash the kale thoroughly and drain well. Trim away the tough central stalks and chop the leaves, if large.

Melt the butter with a little olive oil, to prevent it burning. When all is foaming nicely, throw in the garlic and cook for a minute or so. Now add the kale, turning over to coat in the butter. Cook, stirring now and then, until wilted. Season generously with salt and pepper, finishing with a generous grating of nutmeg.

APPLES

Worcester Pearmain delicately blushed pink early apple with a hint of strawberry flavour

Laxton's Superb a late Victorian dessert apple with a firm texture and sweet taste

Bramley's Seedling the UK's favourite cooking apple has a sharp, acidic taste when raw. However, it cooks down to a beautifully smooth, balanced purée

Egremont Russet crisp when freshly picked, with a good balance of sweetness and acidity

Cox's Orange Pippin a very well-known English apple with an orange-red hue, an intense but sweet flavour and a crisp texture

Blenheim Orange primarily grown as a cooking apple, when it forms a firm purée, this also has good eating properties, especially with cheese

WINTER SQUASH & Pumpkins

Honey Bear an acorn squash variety with deep green skin and firm orange flesh. Ideal to bake, stuff, or make soup with

Butternut squash or butternut pumpkin, has sweet, firm, orange flesh. Roasts beautifully

Baby Bear mini pumpkin that makes an ideal single serving and roasts well to eat as is, or forms a good, edible soup bowl

Crown Prince gorgeous blue-grey-green skin and intense orange flesh which roasts and purées exceptionally

Spaghetti squash steam or bake with butter and cheese, then tease out the light, spaghetti-like flesh and serve as 'pasta'

Festival squash lovely, striped and speckled skin. The sweet orange flesh is ideal for baking or stuffing

BLACK GRAPE JELLY WITH
MUSCAT SABAYON

**MAKES 8 JELLIES AND
ANOUGH SABAYON FOR
EACH**
PREP 20 MINUTES, PLUS AT
LEAST 5 HOURS CHILLING
COOK ABOUT 15 MINUTES

FOR THE JELLIES

4 tbsp caster sugar

1.2 litres chilled black or red
grape juice

14 gelatine leaves or 4½ tsp
gelatine granules

200ml sweet muscat wine

small bunch of black grapes,
halved, to serve (optional)

FOR THE SABAYON

6 egg yolks

100ml sweet muscat wine

4 tbsp golden caster sugar

200ml double cream, lightly
whipped

THIS IS A DESSERT – FOR IT IS A DESSERT, RATHER THAN
A PUDDING – TO PREPARE COMPLETELY AHEAD OF TIME.
The jellies a day or so in advance and the sabayon on the night
before, or, ideally, first thing in the morning. You only have to spoon
the chilled sabayon over the none-too-sweet jellies before eating.
Daylesford Organics grape juice is a beaut. It's deep and dark and
clear and leaves you with handsome glass bottles once the juice has
gone. Do, of course, juice your own grapes should you have a glut
of beauties on your hands (in which case, I'm incredibly jealous),
otherwise, a good-quality, bought juice will be fine and dandy.
A sweet muscat with its notes of orange blossom goes into both
sabayon and jelly, but you could use any sweet wine you have to
hand. A Tokaji, perhaps?
Accompany with some crisp or shortbread-y biscuits, if you wish,
but I am taken by this cool jelly and feather-light sabayon unsullied
and unchaperoned.

Start with the jellies. In a saucepan set over a low heat, warm the
sugar in 100ml of the grape juice and 200ml water, until dissolved
and steaming but not boiling. Meanwhile, soak the gelatine leaves
(if using) in cold water for three minutes until soft. Squeeze the
water out with your hands and stir into the hot juice until completely
melted. (If you are using gelatine granules or powder, sprinkle evenly
over the panful of hot juice and stir to dissolve.) Gradually add the
remaining cold grape juice and the wine, stirring as you do so. Pour
into eight small (about 200ml capacity) serving bowls or cups and
leave to cool completely, then cover and refrigerate for at least five
hours or overnight to set.

To make the sabayon, whisk the egg yolks, 2 tbsp of the muscat
and all of the sugar in a heatproof bowl set over, but not touching,
a saucepan of simmering water. I use a handheld electric whisk
for this, but it's perfectly possible with an arm-powered one. Keep
whisking for about 10 minutes, until the mixture is thick and pale in
colour. Remove from the heat and whisk in the remaining muscat,
followed by the cream. Whisk briefly every now and then as the
mixture cools, then cover and chill for up to four hours, until needed.
Serve the jellies and sabayon with the halved grapes, if you like.

FIREPIT NIGHT FOR 8-10

FOR THE EARLY EVENING: | **MELTED RACLETTE BOWLS WITH PUMPKIN SALSA** | *Olive pressers' soup* | **AFTER FIREWORKS AND FIREPITS:** | STUFFED FIREPIT VENISON WITH ROAST PEAR, PORT SAUCE AND PERFECT MASH | **HOT PEAR AND RUM PUNCH** STICKY DATE AND GINGER CAKE

No late-autumn revelry is complete without a bonfire, but if you have an area of garden or field in which to build a firepit, you will benefit from both outdoor fire and oven in one.

Building, and cooking in, the pit is incredibly rewarding, and it's actually pretty easy to construct, despite requiring spade work. Quite apart from the theatre and fun of it all, the firepit imbues the meat, fish and vegetables cooked in it with a smoky note, rendering them juicy and tender. (Detailed instructions on building the pit can be found on pages 140–141.) Gather a group to share the digging – nothing wrong with working for your supper – and you'll have a pit that can be used time and again. If you are nervous about cooking underground, dig the pit a few days beforehand and have a trial run with a leg of lamb. If you err on the side of gentle the first time (definitely preferable to over-zealous heat), the meat can always be finished off in a low oven. Rain on the night won't be a problem as long as it starts after supper has been buried...

In its entirety, this celebratory menu will serve eight so very generously that I encourage you to keep the quantities the same for 10 guests. If making one of the recipes on its own, reckon on it serving eight. Whatever the numbers, there is rather too much food here to constitute supper in one sitting. It's a real feast, and one that can be prepared in stages, starting a few days ahead. The raclette and soup are intended as an early evening re-fuel, once the pit has been dug and lit. The fire can burn down to embers while you eat. Bury the venison and leave it to cook as you marvel at fireworks, light some sparklers and enjoy the party for a couple of hours, then uncover the firepit in time for a late supper.

MELTED RACLETTE BOWLS
WITH PUMPKIN SALSA

THIS IS GLORIOUSLY EASY FOOD FOR A CROWD if you make the sweet-salty-sour salsa in advance (up to three days ahead is fine). Should the cheese cool down too much to scoop while you're eating, putting the bowls back into the oven for a few minutes will restore them to molten goodness.

Preheat the oven to 200°C/fan 180°C/400°F/gas mark 6. Divide the peppers, pumpkin and about one-quarter of the oregano between two roasting trays and douse each pile with a little oil to coat, saving at least 2 tbsp for the finished salsa. Season generously and roast for 50 minutes, until browned and sticky. Set aside to cool.

Toast the pine nuts in a dry frying pan, shaking often, until golden. Combine with the pumpkin mixture and the remaining salsa ingredients, including the remaining oil and oregano, and season well. Taste; the flavours should be bouncy and pronounced, so add a splash more vinegar and/or more black pepper if you feel it needs it. You can make this a couple of days in advance and keep it in the refrigerator; return to room temperature before eating.

Reduce the oven temperature to 190°C/fan 170°C/375°F/gas mark 5. Slice the cheese thickly – rind and all – and divide between about four ovenproof bowls or dishes. Cook for eight to 10 minutes, until the cheese is melted and bubbling at the edges. Spoon the salsa straight on to each bowl of cheese and serve with the breads for dipping and scooping. You might want to warn people, restaurant-style, that the bowls will be hot.

SERVES 8–10
PREP 20 MINUTES
COOK ABOUT 1 HOUR

FOR THE SALSA
2 yellow and 2 orange peppers, deseeded and diced
1kg firm-fleshed pumpkin or squash, peeled, deseeded and finely diced
leaves from 4 sprigs of oregano, chopped
about 6 tbsp extra virgin olive oil
3 tbsp pine nuts
splash of good balsamic vinegar, or to taste
50g green olives, stoned and roughly chopped
1 small garlic clove, crushed

FOR THE RACLETTE BOWLS
800g raclette cheese
rustic Italian breads or flatbreads, to serve

OLIVE PRESSERS' SOUP

SERVES 8–10
PREP 30 MINUTES, PLUS
  OVERNIGHT SOAKING IF
  USING DRIED BEANS
COOK ABOUT 2½ HOURS, IF
  USING DRIED BEANS

400g dried haricot or borlotti
  beans, or 3 x 400g cans of the
  same, drained
bouquet garni of fresh bay,
  thyme and rosemary
100g smoked bacon lardons
  (optional)
1 tbsp olive oil (optional)
700g kale or Savoy cabbage
300g firm-fleshed pumpkin
  or squash, peeled
  and diced
1 large carrot, scrubbed
  and diced
1 fennel bulb, trimmed and diced,
  fronds reserved and chopped
1 celery stick, sliced
4 potatoes, diced
generous handful of mixed soft
  herbs, roughly chopped
extra virgin olive oil
1 tbsp tomato purée
8-10 thick slices of rustic bread
1 garlic clove, halved

A SOUP FOR OLIVE GATHERING AND PRESSING, WINTRY WALKS… or for rewarding sterling pit-digging efforts. This is a sturdy, ribollita-like affair, not blessed with stunning looks but far more distinguished than its humble ingredients would suggest. Cook it two or three days in advance to make life simpler, and to deepen the soup's character. When it comes to herbs, I use a mixture of basil and parsley with a touch of sage and thyme. Use whatever you have to hand, but go easy with the more dominant, woody herbs. Obviously, leave out the bacon to make this suitable for vegetarians. I make no apology for using pumpkin or squash twice in one menu; seasonal ingredients are there to be celebrated, and one large pumpkin or squash will provide for both salsa and soup.

If you are using dried beans – and it is worth the extra fuss – soak them overnight in plenty of cool water. Drain, rinse and drain again. In a large pan, generously cover the beans with cold water, add the bouquet garni and bring to the boil, skimming off any scum that rises to the surface. Cover and simmer for 1–1½ hours, or until tender. This very much depends on the age of your beans and the soaking time, so be prepared to test after 40 minutes or cook them for far longer. Remove one-third of the cooked beans with a slotted spoon and set aside for a later stage.

In another large saucepan, frazzle the bacon in the oil (if using) until browned. Add the beans (not the reserved third) and their liquid, the kale, pumpkin, carrot, fennel bulb and fronds, celery, potatoes, herbs, glug of extra virgin olive oil, tomato purée and seasoning. Add enough extra water, if needed, to cover the ingredients by 2cm.

Bring to the boil, partially cover and simmer for 1½ hours, stirring now and then, until the beans begin to break down. Add the reserved beans and turn off the heat. The texture should be very thick, but do add a little more water if you feel the soup needs it. At this stage the soup can be cooled and chilled for up to three days.

Toast or griddle the bread until very well coloured, even charred in places. Scrape each surface with the cut sides of the garlic clove.

Divide the toast between warmed bowls, sprinkle with extra virgin olive oil and ladle the soup over. Serve straightaway or cover each bowl with foil and leave in a warm (not hot!) oven for 30 minutes.

STUFFED FIREPIT VENISON
WITH ROAST PEAR, PORT SAUCE AND PERFECT MASH

FOR ITS SHEER SIZE, A LARGE LEG OF VENISON IS A PRETTY GOOD BUY; taking the quality and sustainability of venison in Britain into account, the value is excellent and will allow you to feed a large crowd with style. For safety, please use a meat thermometer after cooking, especially with a firepit, inserting it into the thickest part and waiting for 20 seconds. It should read 50°C for rare, 60°C for medium-rare (70°C upwards is well done); though a couple of degrees either side is fine.

For the stuffing, gently fry the onion in the butter for 10 minutes, until soft and beginning to colour. Add the garlic, pears and herbs and cook for five minutes more. Remove from the heat and stir in the breadcrumbs, walnuts and lemon zest with plenty of seasoning. Stir in the egg after a few minutes, when the stuffing has cooled slightly. Cover and chill. Return to room temperature before using.

To make the sauce, use a large saucepan to fry the shallots or red onion in the oil and half the butter for 10-15 minutes, stirring often, until very soft and turning golden. Now add the rosemary and port, bring up to a brisk boil and cook until reduced by half. Add the stock and boil again, until the sauce has reduced by two-thirds. Taste and season if needed, it should be slightly syrupy. Cool, cover and chill for up to three days. Reheat gently when needed, whisking the remaining cubes of butter in one by one until the sauce is shiny.

Open the venison out on a board and spoon the stuffing down the centre. Roll the stuffed venison as tightly as possible from one long side, to enclose the stuffing and make a fat sausage. Tie in place firmly and at even intervals, with about eight lengths of string. Arrange the parma ham in a large rectangle of overlapping slices, sit the venison on one edge and roll up in the ham. Now lay out a large sheet of baking parchment and put the sage on top. Sit the venison on top of this and wrap up tightly, twisting the ends like a Christmas cracker.

This is where it is sensible to move the operation outside, near to a hose or outdoor tap. Take a couple of sections of last weekend's broadsheet newspaper, separate them into layers of two or three pages and soak them – and I mean thoroughly soak – with water. Wrap each wetted layer around the venison, finishing with a further slosh of water.

SERVES 8–10
PREP 1½ HOURS
COOK 2½ HOURS, PLUS RESTING

FOR THE STUFFING
1 large red onion, chopped
75g unsalted butter
3 garlic cloves, finely chopped
3 pears, cored and diced
2 tbsp finely chopped rosemary leaves
5 sage leaves, shredded
100g soft white breadcrumbs
50g walnuts, chopped
finely grated zest of 1 unwaxed lemon
1 egg, beaten

FOR THE PORT SAUCE
400g shallots or red onion, finely sliced
1 tbsp olive oil
60g unsalted butter, chilled and diced
1 large sprig of rosemary
800ml port
1 litre good brown venison, beef or chicken stock

FOR THE VENISON
3kg leg of venison, boned out
18 slices parma ham
bunch of sage

FOR THE ROAST PEARS
6 firm Conference pears
handful of sprigs of rosemary
50g unsalted butter, softened

CONT...

NO FIREPIT...?

If you don't have a firepit to hand, worry not. You can use a Weber-style barbecue, or this recipe will be as successful, albeit a little less smoky, when cooked in a hot oven. To do this, lay the stuffed and ham-swaddled venison in your largest, oiled roasting tin, tuck in just a few sage leaves, and cover with buttered foil. Roast in a preheated oven at 160°C/fan 140°C/325°F/gas mark 3 for 14 minutes per 500g for medium rare (that's basically 1 hour 25 minutes for a 3kg joint). A joint this size will need an extra 20 minute blast at a higher temperature. To do this, remove the foil and increase the oven temperature to 200°C/fan 180°C/400°F/gas mark 6. Rest the meat for a good 20 minutes, tented with foil, before slicing.

If you have followed the firepit instructions on pages 140–141, the embers should be white and ashen and glowing in places, with no hint of flame. Carefully place your wet logs on the coals and cover with the metal grate. Lay the venison parcel on this, balance the sheet of metal above and cover with earth as directed.

Leave to cook for 1 hour 20 minutes for a 3kg joint (that's 15 minutes per 500g, allowing for 10 minutes' digging time). With any luck, the meat will be medium-rare. Then, wearing protective gloves, dig up and retrieve the venison to much applause.

If you have a meat thermometer, stick it into the venison now and leave for 20 seconds. It should read around 60°C. (See the recipe introduction for more detailed temperatures.)

Meanwhile, preheat the oven to 200°C/fan 180°C/400°F/gas mark 6. Slice the pears into sixths, from top to bottom, removing any core as you go. Spread out in a single layer in a roasting tin with the rosemary and butter. Season lightly and roast for 20 minutes, or until softened and turning golden.

Slice the venison thickly, being careful to cut through and remove all the string as you go. Serve the venison slices with Perfect Mash (see right), the port sauce and two or three elegant roast pear pieces.

PERFECT MASH FOR A CROWD

A TRICK WHEN MAKING MASH FOR LARGE NUMBERS: on the morning of your 'do', make the mash, then, when needed, reheat until browned on top and spoon straight from the dish. Ricing potatoes – and I do strongly recommend this over mashing, if you can get hold of a cheap ricer – for 10 at the last minute is to be avoided if possible and the crisp, golden top will be delicious. Choose even-sized, not large, spuds so that they cook at the same time.

Cover the whole potatoes with water in a very large saucepan (you may need two pans), add a pinch of salt and bring to the boil. Simmer for 20-25 minutes, until the potatoes are completely tender but not collapsing. Drain thoroughly and leave to cool for a few minutes. As soon as you can bear to, peel or pare the skin away.

Working in batches, push the spuds through a potato ricer into a mixing bowl. Slowly beat in the milk or cream with a wooden spoon. Add 100g–200g butter, to taste – the amount is totally up to you – beating it in a few cubes at a time, until all is amalgamated. Season with salt and pepper.

Spoon, or even pipe, if you're that way inclined, the finished mash into a baking dish and dot with the remaining 40g of butter. Keep in a cool place until needed.

Reheat the potatoes for 25 minutes at 200°C/fan 180°C/400°F/ gas mark 6 when you cook the Roast Pears (see left). The top should be burnished and golden.

SERVES 8–10 WITH THE VENISON
PREP 25 MINUTES
COOK ABOUT 25 MINUTES

FOR THE MASH

1.3kg medium floury potatoes

350ml whole milk or single cream, hot but not boiling

140-240g unsalted butter, chilled and diced small, to taste

HOT PEAR AND RUM PUNCH

KEEP THE HEAT LOW TO PREVENT THE ALCOHOL BURNING OFF... speaking of which, do add rum to taste rather than adhering to a measly measurement. The kitchen will smell like Christmas after making this.

Heat, but don't boil, all the ingredients together in a large pan for about 10 minutes. Serve hot.

SERVES 8–10
PREP 5 MINUTES
COOK ABOUT 10 MINUTES

4 tbsp ginger or maple syrup

2 cinnamon sticks

4 cloves

6 allspice berries

zest of 1 orange and 1 unwaxed lemon

2 litres fresh pear juice

50ml rum, or to taste

BUILDING *a firepit*

Be under no illusion, building a firepit is certainly a fun and rewarding weekend project, but the digging part is extremely hard graft. I find a pit most suited to cooking large joints of meat, so I reference that here, but you can also use it to cook vegetables; whole potatoes and roots are a good choice. They should be wrapped in layers of foil, with a few herb sprigs enclosed.

WHAT YOU WILL NEED

At least one spade
At least 9 bricks or 4 breeze blocks
A metal rack from a barbecue or similar, no
    bigger than 80x40-45cm in diameter
A bucket of water
Matches
Kindling to start the fire
At least a wheelbarrowful of logs to burn
A rake
A few small cherry or apple wood logs,
    submerged in cool water for a few hours
Protective gloves
A sturdy sheet of metal, about 80x40cm
A thick, old blanket or mat
A tarpaulin to cover the pit if it rains
    before it is dug out

First find a suitable piece of private ground that you have permission to dig up. It should be grass or earth – not rocky – flat, dry and away from overhanging trees.

DIGGING THE PIT

You're going to expend quite a bit of energy here, probably an hour or two's worth, so assemble your crack team of workers. My talents seem to lie in a bit of a dig, followed by a predominantly supervising-slash-directing role. Yours may differ. Working in a rough rectangle of around 1mx50cm, take the top layer of turf off in long, shallow strips, using a sharp spade. Roll the turf strips up, soil-side out, and set aside somewhere sheltered where they won't dry out, ready to replace later.

Dig down to a depth of about 50cm, piling the earth up close because you'll need it again later.

Working in the base of the pit, either mound up a bit of firm earth at either end, or place pairs of stacked-up bricks or a breeze block at each end instead. Balance the metal rack on top, so that it sits about 30cm above the base of the pit. Any closer and the food will scorch. Remove the rack and set aside, leaving the earth or bricks in place.

THE FIRE

Dampen any grass around the edge of the pit with water and remove any long-dried-out plant life that could catch light.

Use dry sticks and twigs as kindling to get a flame going, gradually building the fire up with bigger pieces of wood, until at least a barrow load of dry logs are burning. Over the next couple of hours, you want the logs to burn down slowly, forming a thick layer of dusty-looking, white-hot embers. This is a very important step if your firepit is to retain enough heat to cook meat through gently but adequately. There mustn't be any flames in the pit when you start to cook, or the meat will scorch before it has cooked through.
Sparks may fly out, so keep extra firewood at a safe distance and have the bucket of water on hand to dampen down any dry grass, if necessary.

WRAPPING THE MEAT

Soak at least eight sheets of broadsheet newspaper very thoroughly in water. Tuck any aromatics, such as herbs, whole spices or citrus zests in with the meat, then wrap it in baking paper and then in the wet newspaper layers, which should prevent scorching.

If the meat is very juicy – a boned shoulder of pork or a whole chicken, for example – I will wrap the lot in a double-layer of foil; it offers extra protection and keeps the cooking juices in. The package will gently smoke and cook underground for a couple of hours to many hours, depending on size and type, so I tend to dig the firepit one day, keeping the hole covered with a tarpaulin if it rains. Starting the fire the following day will mean the feast will be ready that evening, but you could just as easily do the lot in a single day. Joints of meat that have a rich marbling of fat to prevent them drying out should not suffer from some extra hours of cooking, so go for large shoulders and legs, rather than lean cuts.

CREATING SMOKE AND COOKING

When the logs are ready, rake them out a little to form an even layer. Lay a few soaked cherry or apple wood logs on top of the fire. Wear protective gloves to carefully lower the rack down until it rests in position above the embers and smoking logs. Sit a couple of bricks or a breeze block at either end of the rack.

Lay your well-wrapped meat on the grill and balance the sturdy metal sheet over it. The metal should just fit snugly into the hole, if possible.

Re-cover everything with the dug out soil, making sure that there are no holes for the heat to escape through. Cover the earth mound with an old blanket, to further insulate the pit.

UNCOVERING THE PIT

Use the spade to dig and sweep the earth away and, wearing protective gloves, carefully remove the metal sheet and bring the meat out.

To revive an evening bonfire, pull the grate out and throw dry logs into the pit.

Insert a meat thermometer into the centre of the joint. This is essential for safety. Firepit cookery is a great deal of fun but is rarely an exact science so, if the temperature reads lower than the minimum temperatures on page 12, put the joint into a low oven to finish cooking through.

Persistence and toil in tending to and building the pit will, hopefully, reward you with an incredibly tender, smoky supper.

STICKY DATE AND GINGER CAKE

SERVES 8–10
PREP 20 MINUTES, PLUS 20
  MINUTES SOAKING
COOK ABOUT 1 HOUR

FOR THE CAKE

250g medjool or hadrawi dates,
  stoned and roughly chopped
100g dark brown sugar
150g unsalted butter, softened
4 spheres stem ginger in syrup,
  finely chopped, plus syrup
  from the jar
2 eggs
250g plain flour
1 ½ tsp baking powder
1 rounded tsp ground ginger
pinch of salt
60g pecans, finely chopped

FOR THE GINGER-TOFFEE
SAUCE

300ml double cream
200g dark brown sugar
pinch of salt
3 tbsp syrup from the stem
  ginger jar
pinch of ground ginger

STICKY TOFFEE PUDDING WITH A KICK OF GINGER. You can't go wrong with this one, it's exactly the kind of pudding that late-autumn evenings demand. Just don't skimp on the sauce, it's essential that it soaks right through the cake.

To get the timings to work when making the whole menu, bake this the night before or in the morning. The sponge will have longer to soak up the toffee sauce, and you can tick off the pudding as well as freeing up the oven for the party.

On the subject of adding salt to sweet things, I find a judicious amount balances out sugar, especially in the case of toffee sauces. It's a valuable rule that south east Asia has known for many years.

Preheat the oven to 180°C/fan 160°C/350°F/gas mark 4. Line a 20x30cm tin with non-stick baking parchment.

Cover the dates with 150ml boiling water. Set aside for 20 minutes.

Beat the sugar and butter together until light with electric beaters or a wooden spoon. Add 3 tbsp syrup from the stem ginger jar. Now beat in the eggs, one by one to minimise curdling. Sift the flour, baking powder and ground ginger over and quickly fold in with the salt, using a metal spoon or spatula. Fold in half the nuts, half the chopped ginger and all the dates and their liquid. Pour into the tin and bake for 45 minutes, or until well risen and firm to the touch.

Meanwhile, make the sauce. Simmer all the ingredients together, stirring until combined. Set aside to cool slightly.

Pierce the warm cake all over with a skewer and pour about half the syrup on top. Leave for at least an hour, or cover and leave overnight. Warm through in a low oven before serving.

Sprinkle the cake with the remaining nuts and chopped stem ginger. Serve the remaining syrup alongside, with vanilla or toffee ice cream.

HELP-YOURSELF NEW YEAR'S EVE SUPPER FOR 16

HOMEMADE PASTRAMI | **CURED SALMON SIDE** | *A board of seeded soda bread, pickles and mustards* | **LUXURIOUS TART OF BUTTERY LEEKS, MASCARPONE AND SMOKED GARLIC** | SPRIGHTLY ROCKET-CELERIAC SALAD | **AMARETTI CAKE WITH FIG COMPOTE** BLACK FOREST KNICKERBOCKER GLORIES

Generously filling a table with handsome and celebratory food, then stepping back, allowing people to serve themselves as they wish, fills my heart with joy. No dishing up, no adorning of multiple plates as if this were a restaurant and not my home, just a relaxed, busy atmosphere, with the odd bit of friendly jostling thrown in.

This is a distinguished, mellow menu, with a couple of seriously impressive recipes to see the New Year in. Time and planning is the key. Much can be – needs to be – made in advance. The salmon has to be started a few days earlier; the pastrami needs over a week; the cake and compote can be made a couple of days ahead. As can components of the tart and the knickerbocker glories. The idea is to get well ahead of the game. If you are making some, or all, of the menu, write lists and sketch a rough timetable, so you know what you're doing and when. I have tried to write the recipes – bar the pastrami – so they are easily halved, or doubled, if you have vastly fewer or more guests. The menu will comfortably stretch to include a couple or so more, so don't turn extras away.

Space is of utmost importance, so beg, borrow or hire an extra table or three. Don't fret if they're ugly, just throw a tablecloth over the top. Smaller tables could house the knickerbocker glories, or stand as a drinks area, to free up some space on the table so it's not too cramped.

Two pudding choices is an indulgence. Though what better time to indulge than on New Year's Eve? You could negotiate this in several ways: choose the one that appeals more (kids, large and small, love a knickerbocker glory; the cake is probably more suited to the grown-ups), or make just one cake and serve along with the knickerbockers. Lastly, you could serve modest portions of cake as a dessert and the knickerbockers at midnight.

HOMEMADE PASTRAMI

**SERVES 16 (10 IF MAKING
LARGE ROUNDS
OF SANDWICHES
WITH NO OTHER
ACCOMPANIMENTS)**
PREP 1 HOUR, PLUS COOLING
AND SOAKING TIME
CURE 8 DAYS
COOK 3½–4 HOURS, PLUS
½–1 HOUR STANDING

FOR THE CURE

350g rock salt

25g Prague powder no. 1

150g light brown sugar

1 tbsp juniper berries, crushed

2 blades of mace

pinch of chilli flakes

4 bay leaves

3cm piece of fresh root ginger,
sliced

4 allspice berries

2 whole cloves

4 fat garlic cloves, bruised

FOR THE BEEF AND SMOKING

2kg beef silverside joint

good handful of sweet wood
chips or chunks, such as apple,
cherry or walnut, soaked in
water for 1 hour

FOR THE DRY RUB

1 tbsp sweet smoked paprika

2 tbsp black peppercorns,
crushed

2 tbsp coriander seeds, crushed

2 tbsp yellow mustard seeds,
crushed (or use mustard
powder)

2 tbsp brown sugar

1 tbsp sea salt

4 garlic cloves, finely chopped

SOME RECIPES LEAVE YOU WITH A KEEN SENSE OF ACHIEVEMENT and this is definitely one of them. Fabulous sandwiches will be yours, and as part of a spread with homemade bread, pickles, salad and cured salmon? You will be popular. The minute amount of sodium nitrite found in Prague powder number 1 gives the finished pastrami its characteristic pink colour and retards the growth of botulism. It is optional though and if you can't find it to buy via mail order or online, leave it out.

Start by making the cure. Place all the ingredients in a large saucepan and add 3.5 litres of water. Slowly heat, stirring, until the sugar and salt have utterly dissolved. Turn off the heat and leave to cool completely, then chill for a few hours.

Trim any tough membrane and sinew from the beef, also thinning any thick plaques of fat. Submerge in the cure, either in a non-reactive pot or bowl, or in a very large, doubled-up and sealable, plastic food bag. The beef should be fully submerged and – in the case of the bag – any air excluded. Leave in the refrigerator for eight days (two days per 500g), turning every day. Then submerge the joint in plenty of cold water and soak for one to two hours. Rinse in a colander, drain and dry thoroughly with kitchen towel.

At some point during this process, make the dry rub. Combine all the ingredients and use straight away, or keep chilled in a lidded container for up to three days, until needed.

When ready to smoke and cook, preheat the oven to 140°C/fan 120°C/275°F/gas mark 1. Spread the rub over the surface of the meat, pressing it in firmly. Some will inevitably fall off, so just scoop it up and pat it on top.

Prepare a makeshift smoker by first sitting a metal rack on the base of a large casserole or wok. I use a smallish, circular cooling rack. At a pinch, you can use a thick snake of scrunched-up foil instead, but whatever you use has to suspend the joint at least 4cm above the base of the cooking pot. Sit the beef on top and fit the lid on, just to check that it fits comfortably. All being well, cut out very large sheets of extra-wide foil. You'll need 10 sheets, stacked on top of each other. Line the wok or casserole with five sheets of the stacked foil, leaving all the excess to overhang the pan all the way around. Use the remaining foil sheets to line the inside of the lid in the same way, letting the excess overhang all around.

Drop the soaked wood on to the base of the pan, followed by the metal rack. Place the whole lot over a medium-high heat. Cover with an askew baking sheet to hold the heat in and, when the wood is hot enough to be really smoking nicely, remove from the heat.

Working quickly, take the lid off and pour 150ml water on to the wood. Lower the beef on to the rack and carefully top the pan with its lid, making sure all the foil is hanging out. Now roll and scrunch all the layers of foil together firmly, sealing the smoking beef in. Slide into the oven and bake for 3½–4 hours. I would give a thick, round piece of silverside the whole four hours, a thinner, flatter piece 30 minutes less.

Remove from the oven and leave to sit, lidded and unwrapped, for 30 minutes to one hour before breaking into the foil. The pastrami can be sliced

and served straight away, or make it a day or two ahead of time and keep chilled. It is best warm, so wrap in foil and reheat thoroughly in a low oven when needed.

Slice the meat thinly and lay out on a board, with the mustards, pickles and bread on the table (see page 153). A few chicory leaves and sprigs of dill eaten alongside will add freshness. Eat within a week, or slice and freeze in small freezer bags; it will keep for up to three months. Reheat gently (a microwave is good), or wrap in foil and warm through in a low oven to retain the moisture.

CURED SALMON SIDE

IF THE PRECEDING PASTRAMI CAN BE POLITELY
TERMED 'A PROJECT', THIS ONE IS AN ABSOLUTE
CINCH. You won't even need to turn the oven on to end up with
a stunning side of cured salmon. I can think of no better, or easier,
food for a crowd.

To keep the smoky theme alive, marrying the salmon with its
co-stars, pastrami and tart with smoked garlic (see page 150),
I have included smoked salt in the recipe below. Though a wonderful
and surprisingly subtle ingredient, the use of smoked salt is entirely
optional. Please use extra standard rock salt if you cannot find, or
have no wish to use, its smoked counterpart.

Pin-bone the salmon, running your fingers up and down the flesh
to detect the bones; pulling any out with tweezers. Sit the fish on a
couple of sheets of cling film.

Lightly crush the dill or fennel, coriander and caraway seeds with
the peppercorns in a mortar and pestle. Chop half the fennel herb
and mix it in, with the brown sugar and salts.

Spread this mixture over the surface of the salmon and wrap it
tightly in the cling film. Place in a roasting tin and chill for three to
four days, turning the salmon over when you remember.

Unwrap the now-firm salmon and wipe off as much of the marinade
as possible. Holding the fish under the cold tap, give it a very brief
rinse. Dry by dabbing the surface with kitchen paper.

If you have room in your freezer, you can freeze the whole side
for a couple of hours, to make it easier to slice. This isn't strictly
necessary, however, and you can just slice the salmon as is. Chop
the remaining fennel herb and sprinkle over the salmon. To slice,
start at the tail end of the fish and work backwards, using a very
sharp knife and cutting diagonally down to the skin and sweeping
away from you, next to the skin, to free each piece. Make the slices
as thin as you like, though I prefer them to be a sturdy ½–1cm.

**SERVES 16, WITH
ACCOMPANIMENTS**
PREP 30 MINUTES
CURE 3–4 DAYS

1.6kg skin-on side of salmon, the
    freshest you can get
2 tbsp dill or fennel seeds
2 tbsp coriander seeds
1 tbsp caraway seeds
1 tbsp black peppercorns
handful of fennel herb
200g light soft brown sugar
100g rock salt
30g smoked salt (or an extra
    30g rock salt)

LUXURIOUS TART OF BUTTERY LEEKS, MASCARPONE AND SMOKED GARLIC

MAKES 1 ENORMOUS TART
PREP 50 MINUTES, PLUS AT
    LEAST 1½ HOURS CHILLING
COOK 2 HOURS

FOR THE PASTRY

225g unsalted butter, chilled and
    cubed, plus more softened
    butter for the tin
475g plain flour, plus more
    to dust
1 tsp salt
1 egg, separated

FOR THE FILLING

pinch of saffron
100ml single cream
12 large, fat leeks, trimmed, very
    well washed and thickly sliced
50g unsalted butter
15g smoked garlic cloves,
    crushed
5 eggs, plus 2 egg yolks
300g mascarpone
60g parmesan cheese
bunch of chives, finely snipped

THIS IS A TART WITH SERIOUS HEFT, but it retains a certain elegance. A rustic elegance, perhaps. You will need a lot of baking beans; more than I had in the house, so I used a couple of bags of dried pulses that had been hanging around for too long.

Giving a weight quantity for garlic may seem odd, but anyone who has witnessed those monster smoked garlic bulbs will understand the sheer size of each clove. I buy mine from uptonsmokery.co.uk.

A note on the pastry: you could substitute 500g bought, all-butter shortcrust and the world would still turn.

Start with a deep, 26cm diameter springform cake tin. Lightly butter the inside of the tin, then dust the butteriness with flour, tapping and turning the tin and tipping out any excess.

Using the pulse button of a food processor, whizz the butter, flour and salt together for a couple of minutes, until it looks like coarse sand. Tip into a bowl and, using a table knife, cut in the egg yolk and just enough iced water to get the mixture clumping. Tip on to a work surface and lightly bring together. Flatten to form a disc, wrap in cling film and chill for at least one hour, or up to three days.

Remove the pastry from the fridge about 30 minutes before needed. On a lightly floured surface, roll the pastry out to the thickness of a two-pound coin. Line the tin, pushing it up the sides and right into the 'corners' with a small ball of pastry. Leave a good overhang. Chill for at least 30 minutes, a couple of hours if you have time. Preheat the oven to 190°C/fan 170°C/375°F/gas mark 5.

Scrunch up a large sheet of baking paper to make it more malleable then line the pastry with it and fill with baking beans, dried pulses or raw rice. Whatever you use, it needs to reach right to the top or the sides could collapse in or just plain slump. Slide on to a baking sheet and bake for 20 minutes, before gingerly removing the paper and beans. Bake for a further five minutes or so, until the pastry looks cooked and 'sandy' but is still pale in colour. Remove from the oven and immediately brush the pastry all over with the egg white, to seal and keep it crisp when the filling goes in. Trim the pastry flush with the tin. The case will keep, well wrapped, for a couple of days.

Reduce the oven temperature to 170°C/fan 150°C/325°F/gas mark 3. Soak the saffron in the cream. In a large saucepan with a close-fitting lid, gently soften the leeks and a pinch of salt in the butter.

CONT...

The heat should be very low and the lid on very tight for 15–20 minutes, until the leeks are very soft but still keeping their shape. Remove the lid, add the garlic and cook for a couple of minutes more. Set aside to cool.

Whisk the eggs, egg yolks, mascarpone and saffron-infused cream together. Finely grate half the parmesan into the custard and add the chives, seasoning generously with pepper.

Spoon half the cooked leeks into the pastry case and – slowly, slowly – pour half the custard over, jiggling the tin every now and then to distribute everything evenly. Repeat with the remaining leeks and custard, finishing by shaving the rest of the parmesan over the top. Bake for about one hour 20 minutes, covering loosely with foil if it appears to be browning too much on top. It should be a pale gold.

Leave to cool in the tin, set on a wire rack, for an hour, before removing the sides. If there is someone with you, get them to help you slide the tart from its base to the plate, prising it away with a palette knife, if needed. Cut into 16 and serve wedges with Sprightly Rocket-Celeriac Salad (see below).

SPRIGHTLY ROCKET-CELERIAC SALAD

A SIMPLE, RAW SALAD TO ADD COLOUR AND CRUNCH and to soothe the beleaguered cook's brow; you can put this together in a jiffy. The dressing can be made a couple of days ahead and refrigerated if it makes life easier. The celeriac can also be pared a few hours ahead; keep it chilled in its bowl of lemon water.

Have ready a bowlful of cold water with four lemon wedges squeezed in, to prevent the cut celeriac from browning. Pare the skin from the whole celeriac, cutting any root remnants away. Cut into quarters and use either a mandolin or a swivel vegetable peeler to shave long, thin slices from each wedge. As you shave the celeriac strips off, drop them into the bowl of lemon water.

Whisk the oil, the juice of two lemons and the sugar or honey together with a splash of water, seasoning generously with salt and pepper. Add a little more oil or more lemon juice, to taste, as you wish. Just before serving, drain the celeriac strips thoroughly, dry out the bowl and use it to mix your salad. Toss the celeriac, rocket and dressing together and divide between a couple of serving bowls.

A BOARD OF SEEDED SODA BREAD, PICKLES AND MUSTARDS

LIGHT HANDS WITH A LIGHT TOUCH produce the best soda bread, so don't overwork or overmix the dough. Now is not the time for kneading.

Using all white spelt or plain flour in this recipe makes the resulting bread a little more polite and refined, but you could go in the other direction, as I normally do, and replace some with the same weight of wholegrain flour. Replace the seeds with a handful of chopped herbs, if you like. Or try adding a handful of rolled oats and topping the shaped loaves with a sprinkle of them.

Generally, I find people to be less sensitive to the gluten in spelt flour, so I tend to use it for large gatherings where the chances of somebody having a slight intolerance (not the same as a full-blown intolerance or allergy!) is higher.

Preheat the oven to 200°C/fan 180°C/400°F/gas mark 6 and line a large baking sheet with a piece of non-stick baking parchment.

Measure the flours into a large mixing bowl and stir with a balloon whisk. This is to introduce air and break up any lumps, instead of sifting. Stir in the sugar, bicarb and salt. Rub in the butter with your fingertips; this will take a while with this amount of flour.

Swapping to a wooden spoon, quickly stir in the buttermilk or yogurt and milk, followed by 120g of the seeds. Mix with a palette knife to form a rough dough, sweeping the flour up from the base as you give the bowl a quarter turn. Don't overwork the mixture or it will be tough, it should be just combined. The bicarbonate will have started its magic so move quickly as you form the dough into two bonny, round loaves. Sit them on the baking sheet and make a deep cross in the top of each with a sharp knife. Gently press the remaining 60g seeds (about 2 tbsp each) over the tops and bake for about 45 minutes, until golden and hollow-sounding when tapped underneath. Cover the loaves with a loose sheet of foil if they are browning too fast. Cool on a wire rack, covered with a tea towel if you would prefer the crusts to soften slightly in their own steam.

To serve, put the loaves on wooden boards, with a bread knife to cut slices (though you could slice them first, if you prefer). Accompany with jars of mustard – wholegrain, Dijon, sweet – and bowls of sweet butter, drained cornichons, pickled baby onions, dill sprigs and fresh chicory leaves.

MAKES 2 LARGE LOAVES
PREP 15 MINUTES
COOK 45 MINUTES

FOR THE BREAD

700g white spelt flour or plain flour

300g rye flour

1½ tbsp caster sugar

2 tsp bicarbonate of soda

2 tsp salt

60g unsalted butter, cubed

940ml buttermilk, or 800ml low-fat yogurt mixed with 140ml whole milk

180g mixed seeds (pumpkin, sunflower, sesame, hulled flaxseed, linseed etc)

TO SERVE

A selection of mustards and pickles, butter, fresh dill and chicory leaves

Homemade, infused alcohol has its charms at many times of the year, especially when there are plenty of ripe summer berries and stone fruits about, but it seems particularly apt around Christmas, when charming cocktails – not to mention presents that won't cost the earth – are much in demand.

There are so many directions in which you could take each infusion, it really is down to personal taste whether you go with sweet fruit, citrus, herb, fire or spice, or a combination. Use the ideas below as a guideline and don't forget ripe fruits when at their best: damsons, peaches and nectarines, summer and autumnal berries in any combination, elderberries, or sweet pineapple (which combines well with black peppercorns). Vodka will carry flavours well without overwhelming them, but you could experiment with other alcohols.

Some, rhubarb for example, will need a little sugar to temper the sharpness, and this should be added to taste. The amounts I have given are merely a guide, skewed towards the lower end of sweet, so taste and slowly add more, until you reach the desired strength.

Start with a 70cl bottle of vodka, nothing too fancy, but preferably not akin to paint-stripper. A middle-of-the-road bottle will do nicely.

You'll also need a large – and scrupulously clean – Kilner jar, or similar. It should be big enough to hold the vodka, plus a little extra to account for the added ingredients.

This really couldn't be simpler to prepare; you only need to add your chosen ingredient(s) to the vodka in the Kilner jar and leave for as long as directed for each. Keep the jar in a cool, dark place and give it a gentle turn every now and then to redistribute the infusion.

The timings I have given can, of course, be altered as you wish, so taste the vodka while it infuses, stopping the process when you are happy with the strength. Add more of the infusing ingredient or leave for longer, if needed. If you feel the results are too strong, dilute with plain vodka.

Once infused, strain the vodka into a large jug, through a fine sieve. Now pour the vodka into sterilised bottles of your choice. Seal or screw on lids and adorn with an identifying label, including the date.

Keep the bottles in a cool, dark place. They'll last for a good few months, though the flavours will not be as bright after a time. Those with a roomy freezer should try storing the vodka there; the liquid will thicken to a slightly syrupy consistency.

A FEW IDEAS:

STRAWBERRY

Ideal for those with a sweet drinking tooth; a Barbie-pink and intensely flavoured vodka.
Hull and quarter 500g ripe, red strawberries, removing white parts. Leave in the vodka for five days, until the berries have turned white.

RHUBARB

A touch of sugar offsets astringent rhubarb, which should be milder in its pink, winter months. Add more or less sugar depending on taste and time of year. This pale pink drop makes a beautiful gift.
Chop 500g rhubarb and add to the vodka with 100g caster sugar. Infuse for six days.

APRICOT OR PLUM KERNEL

Both apricot and plum kernels add a delicious, almond-like note to vodka, not dissimilar to Kirsch.

Crack a handful of apricot or plum kernels (I bash them with a heavy mortar) and add to the vodka. Add a little caster or light brown sugar, if you like. Leave for two weeks, or up to a month.

CUCUMBER

Cool, clean, (dare I say virtuous?) properties.
Slice four large, washed cucumbers into thin rounds. Add to the vodka and leave for four days.

VANILLA

Sweet and beautifully perfumed, in my experience, girls like this one more than the boys.

Split two fat, sticky vanilla pods and add to the vodka. Leave for five days before tasting, then strain or set aside for up to two weeks in total, or until flavoured to your liking. Add brown sugar or caster sugar before or after infusing, if you like.

If you leave this for a month, and add two extra vanilla pods, you will have vanilla extract.

PEAR AND CINNAMON

This makes a great addition to mulled ciders. Replace the pears with apples, if you prefer.

Add three large cinnamon sticks and five sliced, ripe pears to the vodka and leave to infuse for five days or up to a week. Add sugar, if you like.

LEMON

Lemon is always a success and the resulting alcohol is incredibly versatile; like limoncello without the sugar. Add caster sugar, to taste, if you like the idea.

Make sure you include only the lemon zest, with no juice or pith. Add the zest of three large, unwaxed lemons to the vodka and leave for a week.

LAVENDER AND ROSEMARY

A fragrant and rather grown-up infusion. I like this with orange juice or soda, a squeeze of lemon and plenty of ice. Add sugar to taste, if you like.
Bruise two small sprigs of lavender and a sprig of rosemary by crushing them with your fingers to release their fragrant oils. Add to the vodka and leave for three to five days.

CHILLI

A fabulous use for home-grown chillies.
Cut slits in your chillies – about six work well but use fewer if they are fire-filled – and add to the vodka. Leave for four days, then taste; leave for a week for more spice.

If your vodka turns out to be rather too hot for your taste, add sugar syrup and lemon juice to cool each serving or cocktail down a notch or two.

GINGER

You might want to temper ginger's fire with sugar or honey. A touch of lemon zest goes very well too.
Peel and chop a fat thumb of fresh root ginger. Add to the vodka with 50g caster sugar, if you like, and leave for five days, or up to two weeks.

AMARETTI CAKE WITH FIG COMPOTE

**SERVES 8, BUT CAN EASILY BE
DOUBLED**
PREP 40 MINUTES
COOK 1¼ HOURS

FOR THE FIG COMPOTE

3 tbsp light soft brown sugar

3 bay leaves

1 sprig of thyme

12 plump, firm figs, black if
   possible, trimmed and halved,
   plus more to serve

75ml marsala

FOR EACH CAKE

175g caster sugar

250g unsalted butter, very soft

5 eggs, at room temperature

100g plain flour

2½ tsp baking powder

100g marzipan, chilled, then
   coarsely grated

¼ tsp salt

250g ground almonds

3 tbsp yogurt or buttermilk

100g ratafia or crisp amaretti
   biscuits, roughly crushed

FOR THE AMARETTO SYRUP

150g caster sugar

1 vanilla pod, split

3 tbsp amaretto

THERE IS A CHOICE TO MAKE HERE: if a sophisticated cake, studded with ratafia biscuits and soaked with amaretto syrup would be a more fitting finish than knickerbocker glories, double the recipe and make two, with a double batch of compote. If you feel both desserts would go down well, make one cake and cut it into slivers to serve with the compote, before or with the knickerbockers. There will be more than enough sugar to go around.

Any leftovers keep perfectly for a good few days in a cool place; the texture and flavour seem to improve further after a day or two.

To make the compote, scatter the brown sugar over the base of a large frying pan and set over a medium heat. When the sugar begins to melt, add the bay leaves, thyme and figs – in one layer, if possible – cut-sides down. Cook for a couple of minutes, to caramelise the figs, then increase the heat to high and add the marsala, allowing it to bubble fiercely. Turn the figs over carefully and add 150ml water. Simmer briskly until the liquid is slightly syrupy. Leave to cool, then use straight away, or keep covered and chilled for up to four days.

For the cake, preheat the oven to 170°C/fan 150°C/340°F/gas mark 3½. Prepare a 23cm springform cake tin by lining the base and sides with non-stick baking paper.

With the paddle attachment of a food mixer, beat the sugar and butter until pale and light. Add the eggs, one by one, as you beat. If the mixture curdles, add a spoonful of the flour between each egg.

Sift the flour and baking powder over and add the marzipan (separating the strands as much as possible). Fold in with a spatula. Now scatter the salt and almonds over, followed by the yogurt or buttermilk, and fold those in. Lastly, fold in the ratafia or amaretti.

Scrape into the tin and bake in the centre of the oven for one hour, until deep gold and firm to the touch. Keep the oven closed for the first 30 minutes but, after that, cover with foil if it browns too fast.

Meanwhile, make the amaretto syrup. Put the sugar in a saucepan with the vanilla pod and 300ml water. Dissolve the sugar over gentle heat, stirring, then simmer for eight to 10 minutes, until slightly thickened. Remove from the heat and stir in the amaretto. Let cool.

Pierce the hot cake with a skewer and pour half the syrup over. Leave to cool in the tin; it is lovely slightly warm. Serve each slice with three fresh fig halves and the compote. Offer the remaining syrup in a jug on the side. Crème fraîche is also welcome here.

BLACK FOREST KNICKERBOCKER GLORIES

ONCE THE COMPONENTS BELOW AND OVERLEAF HAVE BEEN MADE, chopped or toasted and set out on a side table with spoons and sundae bowls, your guests can form an orderly queue and dive in, constructing the knickerbocker of their wicked dreams. Multiple, small bowls of everything will prevent a scrum and get everybody served quickly.

To get the ice cream ready for easy serving, space scoops out on a couple of baking sheets and open-freeze for up to 24 hours (any more and it will turn too frosty on the outside). Either serve from the freezer, to order, or pile the scoops into frozen serving bowls and put out with the other ingredients. All the components are easily halved, to serve a more manageable eight.

WHAT I PUT OUT TO MAKE 16 SUNDAES

400g pecans, toasted and chopped

300g dark chocolate, shaved or finely chopped

200g white chocolate, shaved or finely chopped

400g crème fraîche, with 2 tbsp brown sugar marbled through

400ml tub vanilla ice cream, in small scoops

400ml tub chocolate ice cream, in small scoops

Chantilly Cream (see below)

Chocolate Sauce (see below)

Cherry Compote (see page 160)

Best Brownies (see page 160)

CHANTILLY CREAM

A nostalgically frothy and just-sweet-enough confection; use it as an accompaniment to any number of cakes, tarts and compotes.

Combine the cream, sugar and vanilla seeds in a mixing bowl. Whip lightly, until the cream just holds its shape.

SERVES 16, AS PART OF THE KNICKERBOCKER SPREAD
PREP 5 MINUTES

400ml double cream
1½ tbsp icing sugar, sifted
1 vanilla pod, split

CHOCOLATE SAUCE

This sauce begins life with a relatively thin consistency, but it will thicken as it cools, retaining its glossiness. Don't skip the salt; just a touch will balance all that sweetness.

Bring everything but the chocolate to the boil with 500ml water, turn off the heat and stir in the chocolate until the sauce becomes smooth and glossy. Put a folded cloth beneath and serve the warm sauce from the saucepan or from a warmed bowl. Heat through gently or blast in a microwave for a few seconds to re-warm halfway, if necessary.

ENOUGH FOR 16 SUNDAES, BUT CAN EASILY BE HALVED
PREP 5 MINUTES
COOK 2 MINUTES

300g golden syrup
150g cocoa powder
large pinch of sea salt
200g good, dark chocolate, chopped

CONT...

CHERRY COMPOTE

IT GOES WITHOUT SAYING THAT YOU CAN make this with pitted, fresh cherries in the summer months, to go with vanilla ice cream.

**ENOUGH FOR 16 SUNDAES,
BUT CAN EASILY BE
HALVED**
PREP 5 MINUTES
COOK 5 MINUTES

4 x 400g cans cherries in
   natural juice
300ml red wine
60g caster sugar
3½ tbsp arrowroot

Drain the cherries thoroughly, reserving their juice. Measure out 275ml of juice (if using fresh cherries, just use water instead), and pour into a saucepan with the fruit, wine and sugar. Bring everything to the boil and simmer, stirring for a few minutes. Slake the arrowroot in a small dish by stirring in a splash of water to make a loose paste. Add this paste to the pan and simmer for about a minute, stirring until thickened. Remove from the heat and leave to cool slightly before serving in a warmed bowl.

BEST BROWNIES

Line a 23x32cm brownie tin with non-stick baking parchment. Preheat the oven to 190°C/fan 170°C/375°F/gas mark 5. Gently melt 200g good, 70 per cent cocoa solids chocolate and 200g unsalted butter together, stirring until smooth and glossy. Set aside to cool slightly. Beat 4 large eggs, 200g golden caster sugar, 150g light brown soft sugar and 1 tsp vanilla extract together in the bowl of an electric mixer (or using hand-held beaters) for a couple of minutes, to give the finished brownies a velvety texture. Sift in 120g plain flour (or, for a wheat-free version, sprinkle over 120g ground almonds instead), ½ tsp baking powder and 20g sifted cocoa. Pour in the melted chocolate and butter mixture with ½ tsp sea salt. Beat briefly to combine and stir in another 100g chopped dark chocolate. Scrape into the prepared tin, reduce the oven temperature to 180°C/fan 160°C/350°F/gas mark 4 and bake for 35–40 minutes, until almost firm in the middle. When just warm or cool (leave them to firm up in the tin for at least 30 minutes before you start wielding that knife), turn out carefully and cut the brownies into 16 bars or 32 small squares. They'll keep in an airtight container for up to four days.

COSY WEEKEND AWAY FOR 6

CRISP SAGE LEAVES WITH ANCHOVY
HUNTER'S RABBIT STEW AND PAPPARDELLE | *Roast banana shallots, manchego and thyme* | PEARS DIPPED IN HONEY CARAMEL, WITH SOFT CHEESE | RYE WAFERS

A truly wintry supper of rich, umami notes and golden tones. You won't need too many ingredients or any fancy equipment... always a bonus in holiday homes, as well as a relief not to have to rifle through forgotten cupboards in your own house.

What to take and what to buy in situ presents a dilemma on weekend jaunts; taking half a storecupboard with you defeats that carefree holiday feeling. In winter, I would suggest a basic kit of good olive oil, balsamic vinegar, sea salt and pepper, with a wine or soft drink that you rate. Don't forget the bottle opener in case there isn't one. It happens.

So that breakfast is taken care of, consider a loaf that won't spoil – such as sourdough – a bag of oats for porridge and a bag of dried fruit that, with honey, water and a cinnamon stick, can be transformed into a warm compote. Unless you're really headed for the back of beyond, buy most of the fresh items when you get there. With luck, there'll be a good farm shop nearby selling local produce, but do your research first. Lugging a cool bag along would be preferable to subsisting on cheese strings from the local garage. With breakfasts and a supper taken care of, if you strike it lucky and the food is good, the local pub can provide sustenance the rest of the time. This is supposed to be a relaxing break.

If you can be organised, the rabbit and rye wafers can be made in advance. But as the weather will be crisp and cold at best, wet and dire at worst, a spot of leisurely kitchen pottering with friends would make for a rather nice afternoon. This gentle prep will pave the way for a pre-dinner sherry with a few sage leaves with anchovy, and onwards into supper. As this is a relaxed evening (and the very idea of a non-relaxed evening has little appeal), there is no starter. The main course and accompanying shallots will be quite enough. And in lieu of a pudding: a rather stunning cheese course. Choose one magnificent cheese and offer it proudly with the honey-enrobed pears.

CRISP SAGE LEAVES WITH ANCHOVY

I SERVE THESE WITH PRE-DINNER DRINKS AND PRETEND TO BE SOPHISTICATED. Honestly, you wouldn't think morsels of salty fish and sage could be this delicious, but they can and they are.

Smoked anchovies in olive oil can be found in suitably swanky delis or online. I couldn't resist. But the standard, unsmoked fillets in oil are just dandy too.

Sandwich a piece of anchovy between two similarly sized sage leaves, pressing down firmly.

Season the flour generously with black pepper and a little salt. Holding the parcels together, dip them in the flour, coating each side lightly; it will stick, as the leaves are slightly furry and the anchovy will have spilt a little oil. Dip them in the egg, shaking off excess, then back into the flour, again shaking off the excess.

Heat enough oil to cover generously the base of a large frying pan. Add the sage parcels – they should sizzle immediately – and fry for a minute on each side, or until golden and crisp. Remove to a plate lined with kitchen paper to drain briefly. Serve while hot and crisp.

MAKES 18
PREP 10 MINUTES
COOK 5 MINUTES

6 smoked or good-quality
   anchovy fillets in olive oil,
   drained, each cut into 3
36 sage leaves
4 tbsp plain flour
1 egg, beaten
mild olive oil

Warming winter breakfast ideas

If you prefer a mildly sweet breakfast, this **SIMPLEST BANANA BREAD** only takes a few minutes to mix, and you can tart it up with added chocolate chips, cocoa nibs, coconut shreds, crushed walnuts or pecans and/or maple syrup instead of sugar. The addition of coffee here – or dark rum if you prefer – brings out the banana flavour magnificently, as does a pinch of ground cinnamon or freshly grated nutmeg.

Use a fork to mash four very ripe, medium-sized bananas with 75g melted unsalted butter or light olive oil, 2 tbsp espresso or very strong black coffee, 150g brown sugar, one egg, a pinch of salt and a few drops of vanilla extract, if you have it, mixing with a wooden spoon. Now quickly fold in 1 tsp bicarbonate of soda and 210g sifted plain flour, plus any extras you might be adding. Pour into a 1kg loaf tin and bake at 180°C/fan 160°C/350°F/gas mark 4 for 50 minutes or so, until risen and firm. Cool on a wire rack and serve, sliced into 10–12 pieces, plain, or with butter and extra sliced banana.

To start with a regretful negative, grilling **KIPPERS** will, let's say 'scent', the kitchen and probably the rest of the house. On a more positive note, a buttered and grilled kipper is so delicious that I often wonder why they aren't more popular.

Top the kippers, skin-side down on a baking sheet, with a few dots of unsalted butter, and slide under a hot grill until golden and crisp in places. Mashing a little crushed garlic and chopped parsley or chives into the soft butter before grilling is recommended, but may not suit everyone's breakfast-time taste buds. If the smell bothers you, try 'jugging' the fish: place them, tails-up, in a very large jug, and fill it with just-boiled water. Set aside for eight to nine minutes until thoroughly heated through, then drain well. Serve with scrambled eggs, plenty of black pepper and a generous wedge of soda bread.

Ripe and quartered pears, apples and quinces will make beautiful **ROAST WINTER FRUITS** when cooked in a low-ish oven the night before; you can reheat them quickly for breakfast. Leave the fruits whole, or halve or quarter if large, and place eight hefty chunks or whole fruits in a roasting dish. Spice every roasting dish of prepared fruits with any combination of whole star anise (just a couple will do), fresh bay leaves, finely grated orange or lemon zest, freshly cracked black pepper and a broken cinnamon quill. Tuck a split vanilla pod in, if the mood takes you. Add mild honey or sugar to sweeten the fruits – quinces will need far more than pears or apples – and douse the lot in half a wine glass of orange juice or, as Skye Gyngell recommends, verjuice.

To cook, cover loosely with foil and gently bake at 150°C/fan 130°C/300°F/gas mark 2 for about two hours, gently turning over once or twice, until glazed and very tender. Just apples and/or pears will take less time, but quinces need to soften slowly until orange-pink. If you only have apples and pears, you can speed matters up by roasting the uncovered fruit at 200°C/fan 180°C/400°F/gas mark 6 for 20 minutes, stirring a couple of times during cooking. Either way, serve warm, with dollops of Greek yogurt and a generous sprinkling of granola, to make a form of breakfast crumble. This will serve around eight hungry breakfasters. A glass of freshly squeezed blood orange juice – in season during the winter – would be a delightful accompaniment.

Surely king of the warming breakfast, *porridge* doesn't need much explaining, though I do tend to use a mixture of oat bran and whole rolled oats these days. Cooking with a mixture of water and soy milk gives a particularly creamy texture, but just water, or any milk, or a mixture, will all do fine. I always add a pinch of salt.

Baked (for preference) or poached rhubarb compote, gussied up with vanilla or orange zest, and spooned on to each warm bowl of porridge, will make a real treat of breakfast for very little effort. Add a few toasted nuts, a little maple syrup or honey and serve with more hot milk, or even thick cream if you're that way inclined.

This recipe for **BACON SCOTCH PANCAKES** with maple syrup will serve six people, working on four pancakes per person. If you don't like the idea of bacon in the pancakes, or have vegetarian guests, leave it out, or replace with blackberries or blueberries in season.

Whisk 250g self-raising flour in a mixing bowl, to get some extra air into it and do away with the faff of sieving. Add a good pinch of salt and 3 tbsp caster sugar. Make a well in the centre and gradually whisk in a beaten mixture of four eggs, 175ml milk and 50g melted unsalted butter. Incorporate all the flour from the edges as you mix to make a smooth batter, akin to thick double cream in consistency. Add a little more milk, if needed.

Grill 18 rashers of streaky bacon until golden and crisp. Drain on kitchen paper and break six of the rashers into three. Keep the remaining bacon warm.

Place a large frying pan or a flat, cast-iron griddle over a medium heat. Brush it lightly with kitchen paper dipped in very soft unsalted butter or a flavourless vegetable oil.

Working in batches, drop tablespoonfuls of batter into the pan, leaving space for each to spread. Immediately sprinkle each pancake with three pieces of bacon and leave to cook for about two minutes, until bubbles break on the surface of the batter and the underside is golden brown. Flip over and cook for a further minute or so. Keep warm while you cook the remaining batter. Serve in stacks, with the reserved bacon rashers and plenty of maple syrup.

Put the storecupboard to good use and make **BAKED CHILLI BEANS**; far more impressive than ready-made versions. The ultimate would be giant Greek gigantes beans but, failing a Greek deli, they can be hard to find, so use cannellini, haricot or borlotti instead. Soak 500g dried beans in plenty of water overnight. Drain, rinse and cover with fresh water in a large pan. Add a bay leaf and half an onion, bring to the boil, then simmer for 40 minutes, or until almost tender. Beans take varying times to soften, so keep an eye on them.

Preheat the oven to 180°C/fan 160°C/350°F/gas mark 4 (or this is the perfect recipe for the roasting oven of an Aga). Drain the beans and transfer to a roasting dish with 250ml well-flavoured vegetable or chicken stock, a chopped red chilli or a pinch of dried chilli flakes, a can of plum tomatoes, two crushed garlic cloves, 2 tbsp extra virgin olive oil, a sprig of rosemary, if you have it, and a pinch of sugar. Season well and bake for 45 minutes to one hour, until the beans are soft and saucy.

You could also dispense with the soaking and simmering and use two cans of drained beans instead. Add 100ml stock and bake for 30 minutes. Thick toast, made from bread with a bit of character, is a must, but a poached egg or a sausage or two wouldn't go amiss. I once had these with a grilled comte cheese and mushroom sandwich and I must say it was pretty magnificent, as breakfasts go.

HUNTER'S RABBIT STEW AND PAPPARDELLE

SERVES 6 AS A PASTA SAUCE
PREP 20 MINUTES
COOK 1 HOUR 20 MINUTES

50g smoked bacon lardons
3 tbsp olive oil
1 large carrot, finely diced
1 large celery stick, finely diced
1 large onion, finely diced
2 garlic cloves, chopped
500g rabbit joints, or 1 large
    rabbit, skinned and jointed)
2 tsp juniper berries, crushed
leaves from 1 sprig of rosemary,
    chopped
250ml (a large glass) of dry
    white wine
500ml good chicken (or rabbit)
    stock
75ml double cream
800g fresh pappardelle pasta,
    or 500g dried pappardelle
manchego or a hard pecorino
    cheese, finely grated, to serve

ONCE TENDER, THE BRAISED RABBIT IS SHREDDED OR CHOPPED AND RETURNED TO THE PAN to form a rich, but not at all heavy, sauce for fresh pasta. Add cream to taste; 75ml is really just a guide. It can be replaced with a generous spoonful of mascarpone for an even silkier finish.

In a large casserole, heat the lardons in 1 tbsp of the oil until they begin to sizzle and brown. Add the vegetables and cook gently, stirring often, for about eight minutes, or until soft. Stir in the garlic and cook for a further two minutes, then remove to a large bowl.

Return the empty pan to the heat with a further tablespoon of olive oil. Add half the rabbit pieces and cook until browned on all sides. Add to the softened vegetables and repeat with the remaining oil and rabbit pieces. Now return the vegetables and all the browned rabbit to the pan with the juniper, rosemary, wine and half the stock.

Bring to the boil, cover and simmer gently for 30 minutes. Fish out the rabbit pieces and lay on a board to cool slightly. Shred or dice the meat when cool enough to handle, discarding the bones.

Meanwhile, add the remaining stock to the pan and simmer, uncovered, for 20 minutes or so, until the liquid has reduced by at least two-thirds. When the sauce seems syrupy, return the rabbit to the pan with the cream and heat through for a few minutes. Check the seasoning and adjust to taste, allowing for the salty cheese scattered over each serving. The stew may be made up to 48 hours in advance up to this point and cooled, then chilled. Reheat thoroughly when needed, with an extra splash of water to loosen.

Cook the pappardelle in plenty of boiling, salted water according to the packet instructions. Drain and immediately toss with the rabbit stew. Serve with plenty of finely grated manchego, as you should have some to hand for the Roast Banana Shallots (see page 170), or pecorino, and eat with the roast shallots.

ROAST BANANA SHALLOTS, MANCHEGO AND THYME

NO MORE PEELING ONIONS! A joy for sensitive – and restless – souls. Sweet shallots roast and caramelise slowly with luscious aplomb and I guarantee you'll make these more than once.

Preheat the oven to 170°C/fan 150°C/340°F/gas mark 3½.

Slice the shallots in half from top to bottom, trimming any hairy bits from the root as you do so, but leaving them unpeeled. Choose a large ovenproof dish or roasting tin, just big enough to hold the halved shallots in a single layer. Drizzle the base with half the olive oil and scatter with two sprigs of thyme. Season with salt and pepper. Tuck the shallot halves in snugly, cut-sides down.

Roast for 50 minutes to one hour, or until soft. Increase the oven temperature to 180°C/fan 160°C/350°F/gas mark 4.

Use a spatula to carefully flip the shallots over, so that they all lie with cut-sides upwards. Drizzle with the remaining olive oil, add the balsamic vinegar and two more sprigs of thyme. Return to the oven for about 15 minutes, until well caramelised. Scatter with the leaves of the remaining thyme and shave the manchego over with a vegetable peeler. Serve from the dish, with the Hunter's Rabbit Stew and Pappardelle (see page 168).

SERVES 6 AS A SIDE DISH
PREP 15 MINUTES
COOK 1 HOUR

9 banana shallots
4 tbsp extra virgin olive oil
6 sprigs of thyme
2 tbsp balsamic vinegar
50g manchego cheese

RYE WAFERS

MAKING YOUR OWN CRACKERS FOR CHEESE IS A
REWARDING, THOUGH COMPLETELY OPTIONAL, EXTRA.
The seeds can be kneaded into the dough rather than scattered over
if you'd rather incorporate them thoroughly, and do use any single
variety or combination that appeals. Finely grated parmesan, dried
or finely chopped fresh herbs, chilli flakes, celery salt, citrus zests,
paprika, finely chopped olives or sundried tomatoes, caraway, cumin
or coriander seeds will all enhance the basic mixture.

Preheat the oven to 210°C/fan 190°C/425°F/gas mark 7, and oil
or line three baking sheets.

Preferably in the bowl of a mixer fitted with a paddle attachment
(a wooden spoon will also do perfectly well), combine the flours
and salt, turn the machine on low and slowly add the oil and 50ml
of barely warm water. Stop adding water when everything comes
together to form a pliable, but not sticky, dough. You may need
another spoon or so of water, you may not. This really isn't a
temperamental mix at all, so slowly add a little more flour or water
as needed to reach the right consistency.

Knead for about 10 minutes, either by hand on a work surface, or
with the dough hook attachment of a food processor. Cover the
bowl with a damp cloth and leave to rest for 30 minutes or so.

You can use a pasta machine for this next stage but, to be honest,
I find it rather a faff and prefer to use a rolling pin. On a floured
surface, roll the dough out, one-third at a time. An even thickness of
about 3mm is what you're after.

Cut into cracker-sized triangles or squares. You can leave them in
elegantly long strips and break them into shards after cooking. Or
stamp out circles or more ambitious shapes, if you wish.

Space each batch of wafers out on a large baking sheet and brush
lightly with oil. Scatter with one-third of the seeds – inevitably a few
will fall off – no matter, bake them anyway and scatter the seeds
over the wafers as you serve them. Bake for eight to 12 minutes,
depending on size and thickness, until crisp and curling up prettily
at the edges. I find they cool perfectly well on the baking sheets.
Repeat to use up all the dough and seeds. Store in an airtight tin for
up to 10 days.

**MAKES 20-40 CRACKERS,
DEPENDING ON SIZE**
PREP 25 MINUTES, PLUS ABOUT
30 MINUTES RESTING TIME
COOK 8–12 MINUTES

60ml extra virgin olive oil, plus
  more to brush
100g rye flour, plus more to dust
50g spelt, or wholemeal, or white
  plain flour
½ tsp sea salt
75g mixed seeds (poppy, linseed,
  sesame, pumpkin, or sunflower,
  for example)

PEARS DIPPED IN HONEY CARAMEL,
WITH SOFT CHEESE

THESE PEARS, ENROBED IN THEIR SULTRY CLOAKS OF CRISP CARAMEL, are almost impossibly delightful. A light, mousse-like goat's cheese is what I offer alongside here, but a salty blue or a molten brie would be equally apt; something to hold up to the dark caramel and fruit. Simply choose a single, characterful cheese you love. About 400-500g will do very well for six after such a hearty main course. If, at other times of the year, plump black or green figs are what you have instead of pears, carefully enrobe the whole fruits with honey caramel. They will be equally as stunning.

Cut a thin sliver from the base of each pear so that it will sit upright, then – and this is the important part – stick the tines of a fork firmly into the base of each so that you can pick it up like a pear lollipop. Lay out in a row.

In a large, heavy-based saucepan (large to contain the caramel safely, heavy-based to melt the sugar evenly), heat the sugar, honey, salt and 100ml water together very gently, stirring with a wooden spoon until the sugar has dissolved. Put the spoon aside and increase the heat to get the mixture bubbling steadily. After about five minutes, the caramel should darken in colour and appear thicker. You are after a deep chestnut hue. At around 150°C/300°F on a sugar thermometer, if you're measuring, turn off the heat and immediately take a pear in each hand, holding them by the fork. On NO account should you touch the hot caramel; it will burn severely.

Dip and swirl the pears into the caramel to coat most of the top of each fruit, turning them in the air for at least 10 seconds until set just enough to remove the forks. To do this, gingerly hold the caramel-free base and sit the pears upright. Repeat with the remaining four pears. Serve within three or four hours, so that the caramel coating remains crisp, accompanied by homemade Rye Wafers (see page 171) or bought crackers and cheese.

SERVES 6
PREP 20 MINUTES
COOK ABOUT 15 MINUTES

6 plump, firm-but-ripe pears
150g light brown soft sugar
100g runny honey
pinch of salt

MEZZE NIGHT for 12

HONEY-ROAST BEETROOT AND CARROT SALAD | **STUFFED VINE LEAVES (DOLMADES)** | *Golden cauliflower with a sesame dressing* | **BRAISED CALAMARI** | CHICKEN OR VEGETABLE KDRA WITH ALMONDS AND COUSCOUS | BLOOD ORANGE ICE CREAM | BOUGATSA **FRESH MINT TEA**

This menu should start with a disclaimer: it is in no way authentic. I have magpied from here and there, borrowing influences from Morocco, Greece, Italy and my notebooks to end up with a handful of easy little dishes that complement each other. The idea being that producing a colourful spread of compatible small plates, along with a majestic kdra (a kind of tagine) and a stunning dessert, won't prove too arduous if you spread the workload over a few days.

Of course, you can cut down and simplify: use a bought mayonnaise to accompany the squid; buy your dolmades from a deli, they are usually very good; forget about the bougatsa entirely – it's an extra anyway – or replace it with little squares of bought baklava to go with mint tea... I could go on, but suggesting you buy everything in is rather missing the point of a cookery book!

These mezze recipes will serve 12 as a feast if all are made, but are starter-sized for six if you only do a couple. I throw big cushions on the floor to sit on and lay everything out in the middle, or on a low table, with a stack of serving plates and plenty of napkins. Serve the mezze in little dishes and bulk out with flatbreads and houmous, if you need to. It should be easy to create a feeling of plenty.

The kdra will serve six as a main course, more with extra dishes. The ice cream will serve 12 as a stand-alone dessert. The bougatsa pastries are intended to be sliced or at least halved if served with the ice cream, so the recipe makes six, however, if making on their own, reckon on one whole pastry per person.

MEZZE
HONEY-ROAST BEETROOT AND CARROT SALAD

IF YOU CAN FIND MULTICOLOURED CARROTS AND BEETROOTS at a farmers' market or similar, this vibrant salad is a cracking way to celebrate them; the slow roasting concentrates their natural sugars. By all means, use pretty baby carrots and beets if they have a good flavour... those tiny ones so often don't, though.

Use only as much harissa as you and your guests would like, caution is sensible as too much fire will kill the sweetness of the honeyed vegetables.

Preheat the oven to 180°C/fan 160°C/350°F/gas mark 4. Cut the beets into chunks or wedges a little smaller than the carrot slices; this is not a delicate affair so they don't want to be neatly cubed, just even in size. Toss with the carrots, 1 tbsp of harissa to start, the honey, olive oil and plenty of salt and pepper. Spread out on a baking tray and roast slowly for about one hour, stirring occasionally, until the vegetables are caramelised and a little shrivelled.

Remove from the oven and squeeze the lemon juice over, tasting gingerly and adding more olive oil, harissa or honey as you think right. Leave to cool a little, then stir the coriander leaves through and serve warm or at room temperature.

**SERVES 12 AS PART OF A
  MEZZE SPREAD**
PREP 20 MINUTES
COOK 1 HOUR

500g smallish beetroots,
  scrubbed and trimmed
500g carrots, scrubbed and
  thickly sliced
1–2 tbsp good-quality harissa
  paste, to taste
2 tbsp light, clear honey, or
  to taste
2 tbsp olive oil, plus more
  to dress
squeeze of lemon juice
small handful of coriander
  leaves, roughly chopped

MEZZE
STUFFED VINE LEAVES (DOLMADES)

MAKES ABOUT 26
PREP 30 MINUTES, PLUS
   COOLING AND OPTIONAL
   CHILLING TIME
COOK 1½ HOURS

at least 35 large vine leaves,
   fresh or brined
150g brown long-grain rice
1 large onion, finely chopped
about 4 tbsp extra virgin olive oil
50g pine nuts
2 garlic cloves, crushed
50g golden raisins
handful of mint leaves, finely
   chopped
handful of dill fronds, finely
   chopped
finely grated zest and juice of
   1 unwaxed lemon

MAKE THESE A COUPLE OF DAYS BEFORE AND KEEP IN
THE REFRIGERATOR, returning them to room temperature about
an hour before serving. Their flavours will improve and mellow...
and so should you, for there'll be no need to do any last-minute vine
leaf stuffing. Ideally, you or a neighbour might have a prolific grape
vine to plunder for fresh leaves but, if you get stuck, use blanched
cabbage leaves instead. I have gone for a vegetarian filling but do
add minced lamb, pork or beef if you wish, browning it off at the
beginning with the onion. Any extra dill fronds can be packed into
the baking dish with the dolmades to fragrance them further. I like
the nuttiness of brown rice, but you can just as well use white.

Place the (drained) vine leaves in a large, heatproof bowl and
cover with just-boiled water. Set aside to soak for 15 minutes or so.
Meanwhile, rinse the rice well and tip into a saucepan. Cover with
enough water to reach the first knuckle of your upside-down index
finger when you rest the tip on the rice. Throw in a pinch of salt,
cover with an askew lid and simmer gently for 20 minutes, or until
just tender. If any water remains, drain it off and set the rice aside.

Slowly soften the onion in half the oil, stirring, until translucent.
Add the pine nuts and ramp the heat up a little, cooking until both
nuts and onions turn pale gold. Remove from the heat and stir in the
cooked rice, garlic, raisins, mint, dill, lemon zest and half the juice.
Season with salt and freshly ground black pepper. Preheat the oven
to 170°C/fan 150°C/340°F/gas mark 3½.

Drain the vine leaves and pick out your best beauties; you want
them large and untorn. Use any raggedy leaves to line the base of a
rectangular baking dish. Lay a first-class leaf on a chopping board,
veiny side up (shiny side down) and cut out the coarse part of the
stalk. Don't go too mad, leave the leaf as intact as possible. Place a
scant tablespoon of filling on the base of the leaf, fold in both sides
and roll away from you firmly to create a neatly plump cigar. It gets
easier with practice. Pack the dolmades into the dish, seams down
and as tightly as possible to prevent them unrolling. Repeat until you
run out of filling or leaves. Pour enough boiling water over to just
cover, add the remaining lemon juice and oil and cover with more
raggedy leaves, if you have them. Cover the lot tightly with foil.

Bake for an hour, then remove from the oven and weigh down with
a couple of cans on top of the foil. Leave to cool completely. Chill
for up to three days before serving at room temperature.

MEZZE
GOLDEN CAULIFLOWER
WITH A SESAME DRESSING

IF YOU HAVEN'T TRIED ROASTING CAULIFLOWER, DO; it's so different to the soggy, sad boiled veg.

The sesame dressing can be made up to a week in advance and kept chilled. Bring it back to room temperature and thin it down with water when you need it. The sesame seeds themselves have a mind of their own, so it's safer to toast them separately in a dry frying pan, shaking often, until they are evenly golden, and sprinkling over the cooked cauliflower to finish.

Pour the sesame seeds into a dry frying pan, place over a medium heat and toast, stirring, until golden and fragrant. Remove from the pan and set aside. Preheat the oven to 200°C/fan 180°C/400°F/ gas mark 6. Toss the cauliflower with the oil, cumin, chilli and a generous grinding of salt and pepper. Spread out on a baking sheet and roast for about 25 minutes, shaking occasionally to redistribute, until charred at the edges. Remove from the oven and scatter with the sesame seeds.

To make the dressing, whisk together all the ingredients with 75ml water until smooth. Season with salt and pepper and adjust the lemon juice and honey as needed until it tastes good to you.

Serve the hot cauliflower with a bowl of the dressing to spoon over.

**SERVES 12 AS PART OF A
  MEZZE SPREAD**
PREP 15 MINUTES
COOK 25 MINUTES

FOR THE CAULIFLOWER
3 tbsp sesame seeds
1 large cauliflower, cut into
  small florets
4 tbsp olive oil
1 tbsp cumin seeds
½ tsp dried chilli flakes

FOR THE SESAME DRESSING
4 tbsp light tahini
juice of 1 lemon, or to taste
1 tsp honey, or to taste
1 garlic clove, crushed
2 tbsp extra virgin olive oil

MEZZE
BRAISED CALAMARI
IN TOMATO SAUCE

SERVES 12 AS PART OF A MEZZE SPREAD

PREP 20 MINUTES

COOK 50 MINUTES

FOR THE CALAMARI

4 garlic cloves, finely sliced

2 red chillies, slit lengthways

3 tbsp extra virgin olive oil, plus more to serve

700ml passata (sieved tomatoes) or canned chopped tomatoes

1kg small squid or cuttlefish, cleaned, bodies sliced into rings

handful of parsley, roughly chopped

FOR THE SAFFRON MAYONNAISE

pinch of saffron threads

2 egg yolks

1 garlic clove, crushed

300ml very mild olive oil or groundnut oil

lemon juice, to taste

LONG AND SLOW OR SHORT AND BRISK ARE THE ONLY OPTIONS WHEN COOKING SQUID (kalamari or calamari if you're Greek or Italian. It's a better word, don't you think?). Done right, both result in tender, non-rubber band-like flesh. A gentle simmer, as here, with a bounty of garlic and a background note of chilli, renders sliced squid absolutely tender and comforting with very little actual work involved. (I have also had great success with octopus in this recipe.)

To make it simpler still, you could easily buy a lovely, fresh mayonnaise and stir in steeped saffron stamens and a little crushed garlic to save yourself a bit of faff.

Gently heat the garlic, whole slit chillies and oil together in a large pan, stirring for two to three minutes as the garlic becomes fragrant but not allowing it to brown. Add the tomatoes and squid rings and tentacles with about 200ml water.

Cover with a lid and simmer very slowly for about 45 minutes, until the squid is completely tender. Stir every now and then to check the mixture is not catching. If too much liquid remains (the sauce should be thick and rich), remove the lid for the last few minutes of cooking; if the sauce is sticking, add a little extra water. Season to taste with salt and pepper and remove the whole chillies; at this point the calamari can be cooled and chilled for up to two days. Reheat gently before serving.

Make the mayonnaise while the seafood simmers. Set the saffron and 1 tbsp boiling water aside in a little bowl to steep. Use a food mixer or an electric hand whisk and a bowl to beat the egg yolks and garlic together with a pinch of salt. Gradually add the oil, we're talking drop-by-drop at first, as you blend or whisk, increasing to a steady, thin trickle and continuing until all the oil has amalgamated into a thick, glossy mixture. Stir in the saffron and its water, seasoning with a squeeze of lemon and more salt, if needed. Chill for up to two days before using.

Finish the hot squid with plenty of chopped parsley and a slick of good extra virgin olive oil. Serve the saffron mayonnaise alongside.

Introducing games at a party definitely warrants gauging your potential players. Self-proclaimed hipster or sneery types will find the very idea tedious in the extreme, but I'd wager that even the naysayers would enjoy themselves, albeit grudgingly, if they ventured into parlour game territory. A drink or two for the adults helps enthusiasm levels greatly. Try to keep the feel light-hearted and the momentum swift, both to avoid boredom or fighting and to prevent any forays into cheesy, Brady Bunch territory.

CEREAL BOX

Bring out this game once any post-dinner slump has passed. It's a simple concept, but one that fells overly ambitious males particularly well (unless your male friends happen to be dancers, yoga teachers or gymnasts).

This game works best with six to 10 players; too many more and matters can become long-winded. Sort your group into two even-ish teams if you like, or play as individuals.

Tear the top flaps from an empty cardboard cereal box. Stand the box in the centre of the room. Make sure there's a bit of space available for flailing and falling manoeuvres.

In order, each player approaches the box and attempts to pick it up. The twist being that only feet are allowed to touch the floor and only mouths can be used to lift the box. Any hand, elbow, knee or other body part touching the floor (or box) will result in immediate elimination, so be prepared to bend and fold your body, as needed.

Once everybody has completed – or been eliminated from – round one, about 2.5cm must be torn or cut from the top of the cereal box, shortening it slightly. The game continues as before, knocking out players who falter, fall or cheat as the rounds go by.

When the box is very low, only the most flexible remain in play and methods of getting low to the ground (usually involving the splits) can get very amusing. The winner is the last man in legal play.

REVEREND CRAWLEY'S GAME

You'll need at least eight players for this one – preferably more – and a spacious room.

Get everybody to stand in a circle and link hands... but not with the person to their immediate left or right. Also, each hand must link to a different person. It will take a minute or two to figure out.

What you will be left with is a big, spaghetti-style muddle of limbs in the middle of the circle. Now you must untie the knot, without unlinking hands. This will involve twisting, crawling through gaps and climbing over arms, until a perfect circle is magically restored. Very occasionally, the outcome will morph into two separate rings, but the process is always surprising and entertaining.

Famous

Get all the players to write the names of 10 well-known people (alive or dead, real or fictional) on individual scraps of paper. Fold or scrunch the papers up and toss them into a hat or bowl. Working in teams, start the clock as one team member picks out a name (without showing it to anybody) and attempts to describe it to the rest of his or her team (without saying the actual name). Each correct name shouted out by the team represents a point. The designated team member should keep picking out and describing names as fast as they can for one minute. When the time is up, quickly move on to the next team.

Play until all the scraps of paper have gone, then tally up the scores. Vary this using charades, or by drawing pictures, instead of verbal descriptions.

MAIN COURSE
CHICKEN KDRA WITH ALMONDS

SERVES 12 WITH THE MEZZE,
    OR 6 AS A MAIN COURSE
PREP 20 MINUTES
COOK ABOUT 1 HOUR

2 tsp ground ginger
large pinch of saffron stamens
75g unsalted butter, softened
4 garlic cloves, crushed
small handful of chopped parsley,
    plus more to serve
small handful of chopped
    coriander, plus more to serve
12 chicken pieces, skin-on legs
    and thighs
1 tbsp olive oil
2 large onions, finely sliced
2 large cinnamon sticks
1 litre good chicken stock
2 preserved lemons, quartered
500g cooked chickpeas (or
    2 x 400g cans)
handful of large green olives,
    drained and left whole
100g whole blanched almonds
squeeze of lemon juice

THIS IS ESSENTIALLY A LIGHT AND FRAGRANT CHICKEN TAGINE FROM MOROCCO. I have included a vegetarian variation, along with couscous that is anything but insipid.

Mix the ginger and saffron into the butter with the garlic, parsley, coriander and plenty of salt and pepper. Dab the chicken dry with kitchen paper and spread with butter. Sit the chicken snugly in a large tagine or sturdy pan, big enough to hold them in one layer, and place over a medium heat. Sprinkle with oil and cook, undisturbed, until golden underneath. Turn and fry until golden all over.

Throw in the onions, cinnamon and stock and bring to a gentle simmer. Cover and cook over a low heat for 20 minutes. Cut out and discard the flesh of the preserved lemons, then slice the zest into matchsticks. Add to the chicken with the chickpeas, olives and almonds and simmer for a further 20 minutes. Taste and stir in the lemon juice; the chicken should be very tender. Scatter with the remaining herbs and serve in its tagine or a large dish.

VEGETABLE KDRA
This serves six as main course or 10 as part of a mezze spread. Replace the chicken with 1.2kg scrubbed root vegetables, cut into chunks. Use something with integrity and staying power: carrots, parsnips, swede, peeled and halved shallots, pumpkin, squash and thickly sliced peppers are all ideal. Fry the vegetables and sliced onion in the spiced garlic butter and oil for a few minutes as in the main recipe, then add all the remaining ingredients, reducing the amount of stock to 800ml, cover and simmer for 20 minutes, until the vegetables are tender but still holding their shape.

COUSCOUS
If you're not steaming couscous the traditional way (and I'm assuming you won't), it needs plenty of herbs and zest. To make enough for a side dish for 12 as part of a mezze, or six to accompany a main course, place 400g couscous in a large bowl. Mix in the finely grated zest of an unwaxed lemon, a pinch of saffron, a crushed garlic clove, a little salt and pepper and a generous helping of cubed unsalted butter. Cover by a scant 1cm with boiling, full-flavoured chicken or vegetable stock, top with a plate and set aside for five to 10 minutes, until the liquid has been absorbed. Season with lemon juice, more salt and pepper and two handfuls of finely chopped mixed herbs (mint, parsley, coriander, basil, fennel or dill, tarragon or chervil). Fluff up with a fork, adding a lug of extra virgin olive oil.

PUDDING
BLOOD ORANGE ICE CREAM

THIS IS A TASTEFULLY HUED PALE BRICK COLOURED ICE, not the deep garnet you might expect from darker blood oranges. Its taste is superlative... honestly, I can't encourage you to make this enough. The idea of reducing the orange juice down in order to concentrate it is gratefully borrowed from a Martha Stewart recipe.

An ice cream machine is an investment purchase so, if you can't justify buying one, freeze the ice cream base in an open container which has a lid, whisking vigorously every hour or so to break up the ice crystals. It will take at least four hours to get very thick, at which point you can put the lid on and freeze until scoopable.

In the interests of celebrating the blood orange, serve with more of the fresh fruit, first slicing the pith and zest away, then slicing into discs. You can pile the orange slices into a large bowl and serve alongside the ice cream for everyone to help themselves.

MAKES ABOUT 1.2 LITRES
PREP 20 MINUTES, PLUS AT
  LEAST 4 HOURS FREEZING
COOK ABOUT 15 MINUTES, PLUS
  30 MINUTES INFUSING

8 blood oranges: finely grated
  zest of 2; juice of all 8, plus
  more to serve
580ml whole milk
6 egg yolks
225g golden caster sugar
pinch of sea salt
280ml double cream
slivered pistachios, to serve

You should have about 260ml of orange juice from the eight oranges, a few millilitres either side won't make much difference. Boil the orange juice down in a large saucepan, simmering it gently, until reduced in volume by two-thirds. Set aside to cool.

Mix the zest with the milk in a separate pan and slowly bring up to boiling point, removing from the heat as the surface begins to steam and shimmer. Set aside for 30 minutes, or longer if you have time.

Return the milk to a low heat to warm through. Whisk the egg yolks, sugar and salt together in a heatproof bowl until pale and airy; the whisk – I'd use an electric one here – should leave a ribbon-like trail when lifted out. Slowly pour the steaming milk on to the egg mixture, whisking all the while. Pour into the cleaned-out pan and return to a very low heat, stirring, until the custard thickens enough to coat the back of a spoon. This will take 10–15 minutes; be patient, because scrambled eggs won't make a stunning ice cream.

Strain through a fine sieve into a mixing bowl nestling in a large bowl of ice and stir in the cream. Lastly, add the reduced orange juice. If the mixture is not cool, leave, stirring now and then, until it is. Chill thoroughly, then pour into an ice cream machine and churn according to the manufacturer's instructions. You may need to do this in two batches. When thick and voluptuous, but not solid, scrape into a lidded container and freeze for at least four hours or overnight. At a pinch, the ice cream can be spooned straight from the machine, just let it become a little more firmly set in there first. Serve with sliced blood oranges (see recipe introduction) and slivered pistachios.

PUDDING
BOUGATSA

THESE DELIGHTFUL GREEK CUSTARD PASTRIES, crisp and buttery and perfumed with orange flowers and vanilla, are purely an optional extra. Halve or slice thickly though, as one each will be far too much after so much food. Serve them with Fresh Mint Tea (see right) and coffee, or as part of pudding with Blood Orange Ice Cream (see page 184). They also make a lovely brunch pastry, or a dessert in their own right, in which case make one per person, with poached apricots or berries and sliced peaches in the summer.

MAKES 6
PREP 40 MINUTES, PLUS
   COOLING TIME
COOK ABOUT 35 MINUTES

325ml whole milk
pinch of sea salt
1 vanilla pod, split lengthways,
   seeds scraped out
1 egg and 1 egg yolk, beaten
50g caster sugar
60g fine semolina
100g unsalted butter, plus more
   for the baking sheet
1 tsp orange flower water
   (optional)
finely grated zest of 1 unwaxed
   lemon and 2 tsp of its juice
12 small or 6 large sheets of
   filo pastry
ground cinnamon and icing
   sugar, to dust

Heat the milk and salt in a large pan with the split vanilla pod and seeds. Bring up to simmering point – the surface will be shimmering – then remove from the heat. Whisk the egg, yolk and caster sugar together in a bowl until thick and pale. Fish the vanilla pod out of the milk and pour the hot milk on to the egg mixture as you whisk.

Return to the cleaned-out pan over a low heat and cook, stirring constantly, for five minutes. Sprinkle in the semolina and increase the heat slightly. Keep stirring until the mixture thickens; it will take at least five minutes.

Cut 30g of the butter into small cubes and stir into the semolina custard. Remove from the heat and keep stirring until the butter has disappeared. Add the orange flower water, lemon zest and juice. Cover the surface with cling film to prevent a skin forming and set aside to cool completely, the custard will thicken further as it cools.

Preheat the oven to 190°C/fan 170°C/375°F/gas mark 5. Have a large baking sheet, buttered or lined with non-stick baking parchment, ready. Melt the remaining butter and set aside.

If your filo is in large sheets, cut them in half horizontally before covering with a damp tea towel to prevent them drying out. You should have 12 small sheets. Working one at a time, brush one side lightly with melted butter, lay another piece on top and brush with more butter. With the short side near you, spoon a scant 3 tbsp of cooled custard on to the lower third of the rectangle, spreading it out to form a smaller rectangle of about 8x6cm. Fold the right and left sides in to meet in the middle, then fold the bottom edge up and fold and roll the pastry away from you to enclose the custard completely.

Seal the edge with melted butter and brush the outside with more butter. Place on the baking sheet and repeat to make six pastries.

Bake for about 20 minutes, until golden and crisp. Serve warm or at room temperature. Though best made on the day, they can be made a couple of days in advance and will still be delicious. If making ahead of time, you'll find that the pastry loses its crispness upon sitting and needs a quick blast in the oven to revive it. The filling can be made three days in advance and kept chilled.

Combine a little ground cinnamon with icing sugar (about 1 tsp of cinnamon to 3 tbsp sugar, say) and dust over the cooked pastries before serving.

FRESH MINT TEA

Divide fresh mint leaves between little glasses or cups. Be generous. Cover with boiling water and leave to steep for a couple of minutes. Sweeten with honey for those who want it and stir in a little lemon juice to brighten.

A few more short ideas and hints for laid-back and hearty ways to feed the hungry hoards.

To make a **SUBLIME ASIAN BEEF SHIN BRAISE** with soy, star anise and ginger for 10 hungry souls, you will need the following: 2kg beef shin on the bone; 1 tsp lightly crushed Sichuan peppercorns; groundnut oil; 150g light muscovado sugar (I know, bear with me); 2 thumb-sized pieces of fresh root ginger, peeled and sliced into coins; 5 garlic cloves, sliced; 200ml Shaoxing rice wine; 3 whole star anise; the pared zest and juice of 1 large orange; 1 tsp salt; 300ml light soy sauce. First generously salt the beef and coat with the crushed Sichuan peppercorns. Use a little groundnut oil to sear the shin pieces, in batches, in a large frying pan. Set aside in a bowl.

Throw the lot, including the beef and its juices, into a very large, lidded casserole or stockpot and add enough cold water to cover generously. Bring up to a gentle simmer. Skim off any impurities, then slide into a 170°C/fan 150°C/340°F/gas mark 3½ oven and forget about it for four hours, or until the beef is extremely tender. Ideally, make this the day before and let cool. Skim off the fat and discard the bones. Keep some of the stock back to use in Asian soups and future braises; it freezes well. There should be enough liquid left in the pan liberally to coat the beef shin. Taste and season with more salt or soy sauce, if needed. Reheat thoroughly on the hob and eat with simply steamed pak choi and rice, adorning each plate or bowlful with shredded spring onion. Follow with fresh mango, lychees and ice cream.

This is one I made for 25 of us on Bonfire Night last year and it seemed to go down well. To make **SAUSAGES FOR A CROWD WITH ONION JAM** in warmed baguettes, work on needing three good-quality sausages per person, assuming your friends are as, um, 'enthusiastic' as mine. Don't forget the vegetarians. Roast the bangers in large roasting tins, spaced well apart and turning at least once, so that they brown evenly. They'll need about 30 minutes at 190°C/fan 170°C/375°F/gas mark 5, depending on thickness. You can coat them with a little honey and wholegrain mustard halfway through, if you like.

Warm through some fresh baguettes. Each loaf should be sliced into five, split open and lightly buttered. Spread a tablespoon of Red Onion Relish with Port (see page 91) inside each and stuff with three, or maybe two, sausages and a few rocket leaves. Hand out with paper napkins.

Failing the onion jam, sliced and fried onions or a good bought chutney or ketchup will do nicely.

It's neither desirable nor practical always to make separate options for vegetarians and meat eaters. Most of us could do with concentrating on vegetables a little more and this is **A VERY GOOD SOUP FOR A COLD DAY** indeed. Make it as needed, or a day or so before, ready to reheat.

This makes enough for 10, as a main course or a lunch with bread, and perhaps some Cheddar or goat's cheese.

Roast two sizeable, peeled, deseeded and cubed squashes. I had great success with coquina squash recently – it has very dense flesh, similar in looks and taste to a butternut, but sweeter – homegrown butternuts would also be ideal. Toss the cubed squash with olive oil, salt, pepper and a few rosemary leaves. Roast in a hot oven until caramelised and soft. Meanwhile, slowly soften a couple of large, chopped onions in olive oil in a stock pot; don't rush the onions, allow them time to mellow and gild. Add the squash, a can of plum tomatoes, a sprig of rosemary and enough vegetable stock to cover generously. Simmer for about 20 minutes, then fish out the rosemary and attack the soup with a stick blender, until smooth. I like this thick, but let it down with extra water until it has a consistency you like. Adjust the seasoning and reheat thoroughly before serving.

To go with said soup... A simple soup is indeed a beautiful thing, but if you feel it needs something more, consider making a simple bread dough, such as the base for Herb Fougasse and Fig and Mozzarella Pizzas (see page 34), and turning it into a **STROMBOLI**. After its first rise, knock the basic bread dough back and divide into two rounds. Roll and stretch each ball to form a large rectangle (about 15x25cm). Lay your choice of Parma ham, basil, rosemary or thyme leaves, pesto, tapenade, roasted peppers, stoned olives, capers, torn mozzarella, shaved Parmesan, sunblush or roast tomatoes... etc... in any seasonal combination you like. Roll the dough up from a long edge to form a fat sausage, making sure the join is underneath to prevent it from bursting open in the oven. Leave both loaves to prove on oiled baking sheets, in a warm place and covered with damp tea towels, for about 20 minutes.

Bake at 200°C/fan 180°C/400°F/gas mark 6, for 35 minutes or so, until golden and well-risen. Cool slightly on wire racks and slice thickly to serve with soup in lieu of bread and cheese. The baked loaves freeze perfectly and can be defrosted in the refrigerator overnight and reheated.

Throw together an enormous, warm and wintry (and vegetarian) main course **SALAD OF STICKY ROAST CARROTS, PARSNIPS AND SHALLOTS** folded through simmered farro, barley or spelt with lots of toasted pecans, crumbled goat's cheese, cooked chestnuts and chopped parsley. Dress with sherry vinegar, a touch of honey, a scrape of garlic and a mixture of light olive and walnut oils. Serve with green salad leaves alongside.

If you're after **MORE FIREPIT IDEAS**, look no further than a pork shoulder or two for cooking underground, each wrapped with a generous handful of woody herbs and chopped garlic. This will work almost as well in a slow oven, but the smoke from the pit sends it over the edge. Serve the sliced pork with a salsa verde and roast beets, fennel and potatoes, or, my favourite, with a homemade apple sauce, peppered with chopped rosemary, and crusty white rolls.

If you make a roast, for however many, it's such a good idea to make a **GRAVY IN ADVANCE** and keep it in a jug in the refrigerator overnight. I fry onions off, sprinkle them with flour, then gradually pour in some seriously good stock (use your very best) and a dash of wine. Whisk over a medium heat for a good five minutes until thickened and smooth. Strain into a jug and set aside to cool. This way, all the stirring and simmering has been done the day before. While the meat rests, your gravy can be whisked into the de-fatted roasting tin – over the heat – to warm through and incorporate the flavours of the roast. Remember, you can never have too much gravy.

There's absolutely nothing wrong with turning out a crowd-pleaser. It's a rare Sunday luncher who doesn't love vanilla ice cream, or indeed custard, with **A HOMELY CRUMBLE**. Apple, or apple and blackberry, frequently get top votes, so don't feel you have constantly to reinvent the wheel.

My mother incorporates crushed ratafia or amaretti biscuits into a basic crumble recipe to great effect, and I suggest you do, too. Another of her tricks I always copy is to dot half-teaspoonfuls of brown sugar over the crumble surface and lay a tiny sliver of butter on each pile. The sugar and butter will melt into bubbling pools of toffee in the oven. As a kid, I would sneak to the fridge later and polish off the leftover toffee discs, blithely assuming nobody would notice their absence. They always did.

Crumble topping can be made in advance and kept frozen, ready to use as needed. The raw, assembled crumble will freeze well for a few months, too; bake from frozen.

INDEX

almonds: blueberry, almond and vanilla choux buns 104–6
amaretti cake with fig compote 156
anchovies, crisp sage leaves with 165
antipasti sandwiches 91
apricot and first raspberry lattice tart 58
artichokes: autumnal panzanella 110
  barbecued artichokes with almonds 74
Asian beef shin braise 188
aubergines and summer squash 112
autumnal panzanella 110

bacon Scotch pancakes 167
bananas: banana, date and maple thickie 47
  simplest banana bread 166
basil limeade 82
beef: Asian beef shin braise 188
  beef in betel leaves 16
  homemade pastrami 146–7
  pressed steak sandwiches 91
beetroot: early beets in parcels 51
  honey-roast beetroot and carrot salad 177
biscuits, sesame 118
Black Forest knickerbocker glories 159–61
blueberry, almond and vanilla choux buns 104–6
borlotti beans: baked chilli beans 167
  olive pressers' soup 134
bougatsa 186–7
bread: banana bread 166
  herb fougasse 34–6
  soda bread 153
brik 114–16

cakes: amaretti 156
  brownies 160
  sticky date and ginger 142
  strawberry and vanilla 78–81

calamari, braised in tomato sauce 180
carrots: honey-roast beetroot and carrot salad 177
  sticky roast carrots, parsnips and shallots salad 189
cauliflower, roast 179
celeriac: sprightly rocket-celeriac salad 152
Chantilly cream 159
cheese: antipasti sandwiches 91
  brik 114–16
  fig and mozzarella pizza 34–6
  galettes de blé noir 60
  griddled aubergines and summer squash 112
  melted raclette bowls with pumpkin salsa 133
  roast banana shallots, manchego and thyme 170
  squash and manouri salad 71
cherry compote 160
chicken: chicken and wild mushroom pies 124–6
  chicken kdra with almonds 182
  lemon and cardamom chicken thighs 94
chillies: baked chilli beans 167
  chilli dressing 123
chocolate: baked white chocolate and rhubarb custards 24
  Black Forest knickerbocker glories 159–61
  brownies 160
  chocolate sauce 159
clams, razor 117
courgettes: griddled aubergines and summer squash 112
couscous: Georgina's toasted couscous with green leaves 95
crumbles 189

dabs, brown butter 98
dates: sticky date and ginger cake 142
dolmades 178

dressings: chilli 123
  sesame 179
drinks: banana, date and maple thickie 47
  basil limeade 82
  elderflower vodka 82
  hot pear and rum punch 139
  pineapple and ginger fizz 28
  raspberry crush 82
  spring juice bar 38
  vodka infusions 154–5
eggs: eggs en cocotte with goat's cheese, tarragon and tomato 33
  Merguez sausages, spiced potatoes and eggs 48–50
  poaching 50
equipment 12–13, 46

farro: farro and green bean salad 54
  farro stuffing 53
figs: fig compote 156
  fig and mozzarella pizza 34–6
fish: brown butter dabs 98
  home-smoked trout with caper mayonnaise 66–7
flapjacks, deep and chewy 92
focaccia 74
fruit, roast winter 166

galettes de blé noir 60
Georgina's toasted couscous with green leaves 95
goat's cheese: eggs en cocotte with goat's cheese, tarragon and tomato 33
grapes: black grape jelly 128
gravy 189
green bean and farro salad 54

ham: crisp ham hock and pumpkin salad 123
  galettes de blé noir 60
  smoky pea and ham soup 88
hedgerow foraging 40–1
herb fougasse 34–6
hunter's rabbit stew and pappardelle 168

ice cream: Black Forest
    knickerbocker glories 159–61
    blood orange 184

jam, onion 188
jelly, black grape 128

kale: buttered 126
kippers 166
kohlrabi salad 61

lamb: brik 114–16
    summer barbecued roast of lamb
        72
leek, mascarpone and smoked
    garlic tart 150–2
lemon: lemon and cardamom
    chicken thighs 94
    lemon and rosemary tart 42–3

mango: green mango salad 22
mascarpone, leek and smoked
    garlic tart 150–2
muesli: toasted muesli bowls 37
mushrooms: chicken and wild
    mushroom pies 124–6

oats: deep and chewy flapjacks 92
olive pressers' soup 134
onions: onion jam 188
    pickled red onion and cucumber
        salad 103
    red onion relish with port 91
oranges: blood orange ice cream
    184

parsnips, sticky roast carrots,
    shallots and 189
pasta: hunter's rabbit stew and
    pappardelle 168
pastrami, homemade 146–7
pears: hot pear and rum punch 139
    pears dipped in caramel 172
    roast pears 135–8
peas: smoky pea and ham soup 88
peppers: autumnal panzanella 110
    pumpkin salsa 133
    sweet pepper sausage rolls 65

pies, chicken and wild mushroom
    124–6
pineapple and ginger fizz 28
pizza, fig and mozzarella 34–6
pork: Merguez sausages, spiced
    potatoes and eggs 48–50
    porchetta stuffed with farro 53
    sweet pepper sausage rolls 65
potatoes: Merguez sausages, spiced
    potatoes and eggs 48–50
    perfect mash 135–8, 139
    a picnic potato salad 103
pumpkins: crisp ham hock and
    pumpkin salad 123
    olive pressers' soup 134
    pumpkin salsa 133

quail in honey and five spice 21

rabbit: hunter's rabbit stew and
    pappardelle 168
raspberries: apricot and first
    raspberry lattice tart 58
    raspberry crush 82
relish, red onion with port 91
rhubarb: baked white chocolate and
    rhubarb custards 24
rye wafers 171

sabayon, muscat 128
salads: autumnal panzanella 110
    crisp ham hock and pumpkin
        salad 123
    farro and green bean salad 54
    green mango salad 22
    griddled aubergines and summer
        squash 112
    honey-roast beetroot and carrot
        177
    kohlrabi salad 61
    pickled red onion and cucumber
        103
    a picnic potato 103
    sprightly rocket-celeriac 152
    squash and manouri salad 71
    sticky roast carrots, parsnips and
        shallots 189
    Vietnamese table salad 18

salmon: cured salmon side 149
salsa, pumpkin 133
sandwiches, pressed steak 91
sauces: chocolate 159
    ginger-toffee 142
    port 135–8
    tomato 180
    Vietnamese dipping sauce 16
Scotch pancakes 167
shallots: roast with manchego and
    thyme 170
soda bread 153
soups 188–9
    hearty vegetable 87
    olive pressers' 134
    smoky pea and ham 88
    squash 127
    soup 188–9
stew: hunter's rabbit stew and
    pappardelle 168
strawberry and vanilla cake 78–81
stromboli 189

tarts: apricot and first raspberry
    lattice 58
    lemon and rosemary 42–3
    buttery leeks, mascarpone and
        smoked garlic 150–2
trout: home-smoked with caper
    mayonnaise 66–7

vanilla cream 106
vegetables: hearty vegetable soup
    87
    pickled 18
venison, stuffed firepit 135–8
Vietnamese dipping sauce 16
Vietnamese table salad 18
vine leaves, stuffed 178
vodka: elderflower 82
    vodka infusions 154–5

yogurt, frozen 59

ACKNOWLEDGEMENTS

With apologies in advance for excessive sentimentality and gushing...

Jo at Brickett Davda (www.brickettdavda.com) handmakes the most gorgeous plates, bowls, cups and mugs in the most covetable hues. Her tableware helped to make the March chapter so beautiful. Jo, thank you for your endless patience when I took far too long to return the plates!

Grateful thanks go to Tobyn at Bell Tent UK (www.belltent.co.uk, 07830 355993) for so kindly furnishing us with an enormous bell tent and myriad accessories to glam up our distinctly rustic field. If you need a fairytale tent for a festival or party, Tobyn is the man to call.

Tabitha, Emma and Rahel, we had far too much fun on those long shoot days and you all went above and beyond. Darling Emma, as always, you have done a sublime job with the photos and, as for Rahel? Loveliness personified. Without the Forest House (thank you to Uncle Dan as well) and Rueben and Liberty to model – avec strawberries – the book would have been distinctly lacking. Tab, I couldn't quite believe it when we arrived at Greatham that summer's morning. What an honour to spend a couple of days there with the best girls and your dear grandmother. Thank you for setting every scene with your treasures, reeling off hundreds of jokes in character and for not minding when your birthday picnic was invaded. More beach cricket for everyone next summer, please.

Diana and Oliver Hawkins, for graciously letting us make a bombsite of your stunning kitchen (actually, that was just me) and photograph your secret garden. It was especially advantageous to have both an emergency pork-delivery service and an ice cream machine engineer on site! Thank you so very much.

To Claire Peters, the talented girl with an eye for a layout. You really have done the most fabulous work on these pages and it was a treat to have you along on some shoot days. And a thank you, of course, to all at Quadrille, but especially to Anne Furniss for commissioning the book in the first place and to Clare and Mark, who will no doubt do a sterling job of getting the word out. To the loveliest agent, Elly James and to Heather at HHB for boundless enthusiasm and kindness.

If there is a funnier, cleverer, more patient or harder-working editor than Lucy Bannell in all the land, I will be extremely surprised. You. Are. Wonderful. Sorry for being sappy.

Thanks also to Diana Henry, whose kindness and encouragement have been of great comfort.

The beautiful hen party models who posed so well: Georgina, Ruth, Joey, Lulu, Becky, Claire, Jess and Fliss. You all looked gorgeous, as always. Thank you. And thanks to all my other lovely friends for recipe testing (that includes simply turning up and eating) and for being ever-tolerant of the book-induced absences.

To my wonderful parents Jasmine and David, grandparents Honey and Gug and brother Ian, for your immeasurable love and help, not to mention the fee-free rural locations and the hand-knitted cashmere.

And to Chris. For never minding the midnight recipe writing and the (occasional) bad Pad Thai. You are my favourite.

Editorial Director Anne Furniss
Creative Director Helen Lewis
Project Editor Lucy Bannell
Designer Claire Peters
Photographer Emma Lee
Illustrator Claire Peters
Stylist Tabitha Hawkins
Production Director Vincent Smith
Production Controller James Finan

First published in 2012 by
Quadrille Publishing Limited
Alhambra House
27-31 Charing Cross Road
London WC2H 0LS
www.quadrille.co.uk

Text © 2012 Alice Hart
Photographs © 2012 Emma Lee
Design and layout © 2012
Quadrille Publishing Limited

Pages 15, 31, 63, 85 and 109 © inspyretash-stock

Cataloguing in Publication Data: a catalogue record for this book is available from the British Library.

ISBN 978 1 84949 108 2

Printed in China